I CHANGED MY MIND: MY JOURNEY FROM INFERTILE TO CHILDFREE

LARGE PRINT EDITION

L.A. WITT

ARTIFICIAL INTELLIGENCE

HUMAN POWERED CREATOR

I support the right of humans to control their artistic works.

I CHANGED MY MIND

We've all heard the stories of infertile people who make peace with their circumstances and embrace the childfree life.

This is not one of those stories.

I Changed My Mind is a memoir by romance author L.A. Witt about her journey through a four-year infertility battle, the steadily growing unease that she was heading in the wrong direction, and the epiphany that she really wanted to be childfree.

Over fifteen years on from that decision, she candidly discusses fear, regret, and the reality of life as a childfree woman in her forties. With a decade and a half in the rearview, with menopause on the horizon and no do-overs, was it the right decision after all?

TRIGGER WARNING

In addition to infertility, pregnancy loss is a significant subject in this book. Medical trauma (physical and psychological) is also discussed at length. Some fatphobia as well.

PART 1

INTRODUCTION

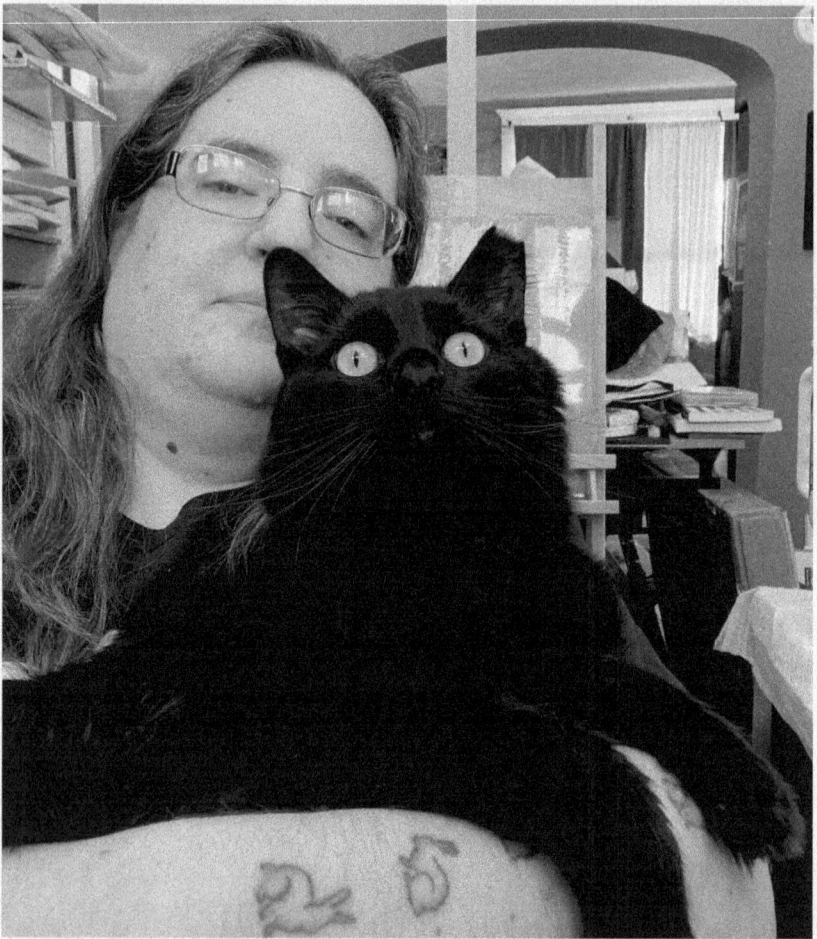
Me with Jason, my writing/painting assistant.

BEFORE WE GET STARTED...

What this book is and what it isn't.

Right off the bat, I want to be clear about what you will and will not get out of this book. First, this is *not* a guide or a how-to book. It's a memoir in which I share my experiences as someone who went through infertility, then chose to be child-free. You might find some of those experiences helpful or relatable in your own journey, or you might not. That's okay.

If you are infertile and trying to make peace with a future without children, and you're looking for a book to help you make that decision or learn how to shift your mindset from infertile to childfree, you probably won't find it here. I mean, it's possible you will—it's entirely possible you'll see yourself and your thoughts and emotions within these pages, and that might help you move forward. You just never know where you'll find something like that. While I would be thrilled if my book does bring you peace or otherwise help you, I don't want to raise those expectations or make those promises. They are not the intent of this book.

This is not an us vs. them book. It's not an attempt to persuade anyone they should or should not be childfree. It is, quite simply, a recounting of my own experiences and how they led me to who and where I am today.

Also, there will be random photos from my life because this is a memoir and I want to.

Eddie and me outside a Pittsburgh Penguins game, behaving like mature adults.

Why am I telling this story?

Over the years, I've heard and read a lot of stories from people discussing the transition from infertility to a childfree life, but I have yet to find one I can truly relate to. All those that I've heard have been about accepting that infertility is here to stay and biological children aren't happening. People either can't afford to adopt or choose not to for any number of reasons, and thus, their future is one without children. Rather than being childless, they've chosen to embrace the hand they've been dealt and be happily childfree.

These stories are perfectly valid, of course! In fact, it's great that people share these stories, and I hope they continue to do so.

But the story I *haven't* seen is one like mine. In mine, infertility didn't make the decision—*I* did. I didn't give up. I didn't decide to make peace with being infertile. In fact, after almost four years of various treatments, especially with some glimmers of hope that they were starting to work, it's entirely possible I ultimately could have had biological kids.

I didn't surrender to infertility. I literally said to myself, "What am I doing? I don't want this!"

That's the key: **I didn't give up—I changed my mind.**

Ironically, people still insist to this day that I'll change my mind about being childfree, and they get very Surprised Pikachu when I tell them I *did* change my mind. More on that later.

So that's the story I want to tell—about fighting the fight of infertility, only to realize that the end goal was something I no longer wanted. I want to talk about the guilt and the relief, the shame and the elation, and the difference in my reactions to finding out I was pregnant vs. releasing myself from the pressure of getting pregnant again.

Not everyone will be able to relate to my story, and that's okay. Hopefully, if you can relate, you feel seen and understood. If you can't relate, then I hope you'll still come along for the ride and find out what life is like for one person who went through infertility and came out childfree.

Also, I'll keep the TMI to a minimum wherever possible. I try to be as open and candid as I can about my experiences, but not everything is for public consumption. Most names have been changed for privacy, and I have deliberately obscured identities or left out some stories entirely if they would cause family conflict, create embarrassment or blowback against someone, or potentially get me into legal hot water. Only people who know me will likely notice those missing pieces, but I'm mentioning it here in the name of full transparency. I'm telling my story, but out of respect and necessity, I'm not telling my *whole* story.

And finally, my husband, Eddie, changed his mind, too. Most of what I talk about in this book will be my own thought processes, what drove me to make my decision, etc., not because I didn't take him into consideration, but because his thoughts and emotions are his story to tell, not mine.

Eddie in his natural habitat:
the kitchen.

Who am I and how did I get here?

It's mid-2024. I'm writing in the place where I work every day: the couch in my living room in a rental house in Pittsburgh, Pennsylvania. It's a room filled with evidence of the life Eddie and I have lived together. Shelves are lined with souvenirs from the years we spent living on Okinawa and later Spain, as well as our travels to Morocco, the U.K., Austria, Finland, and myriad other places.

One wall of the living room is covered with Pittsburgh

Penguins hockey memorabilia. On another, paintings I've created over the last few years hang beside wedding photos and Eddie's collection of Star Wars light sabers.

On the mantel, between two display cases full of hockey pucks, are about a dozen of the books I've written and published, and above them is a plaque—the Romance Writers of America's Centennial Award, given when an author publishes 100 books. Eddie's two Master's degrees hang on one wall. My various writing awards occupy a shelf in a curio case. There's a drumstick I caught at a Bastille concert in Boston in 2017. Behind that, a photo of us goofing around at Medieval Times in California in 2014.

You could say we have eclectic taste.
Dragon statue from Okinawa, Skull from
Kutna Hora, Centurion helmet from U.K.

There is a lot of history on these walls and shelves. A lot
of living that's happened in twenty-two years, especially in
the sixteen since we became decidedly childfree.

Most of that life did not exist when my story, such as it is
in this book, began. Most of that life and those experiences—
most of this reality—is the byproduct of the major turning
point around which this book revolves. I'm writing from a

future that the much younger me could not have foreseen as she set the wheels in motion.

The story I tell within these pages began in 2003, but first, let me go a little further back to who I was in the years leading up to that.

I grew up in the 1980s and 1990s in Woodinville, a suburb of Seattle. If you've ever had Chateau Ste Michelle wine, you've had wine from Woodinville. Back then, there were two big wineries. These days, the whole town has basically been turned into wine country, with tasting rooms and wineries of every size everywhere you turn. I don't drink wine, but that's my hometown's claim to fame, so there it is.

I was raised in a strange little gray area between suburbia and rural farmland. We had horses, dirt trails, and forests to play in, but we were also only about fifteen minutes from town and maybe forty minutes from Seattle. It was a small town by Washington standards, but not one of those one-horse towns of 200 people where everybody knows everybody's business. Basically, I lived on a small farm, but my graduating class had 400 people in it; it was a nice mix of city and country life.

My formative years also straddled a fuzzy line between the life of a civilian and that of a military brat. I never lived in base housing. We didn't move around (I literally lived in the same house until I was twenty-two). But my dad was a reservist and a not insignificant portion of each generation of my extended family spent time in the military. My grandmother legitimately thought it was an act of rebellion when I tried to join the Peace Corps because "we are a proud *military* family!" if that tells you anything.

So I didn't have all the upheaval and chaos of a military upbringing, and I didn't spend a ton of time on/around bases, but I had more familiarity with military life than other kids I grew up with.

In 2002, about three years after I graduated high school, I met Eddie, a Sailor stationed aboard a ship in Bremerton. We dated and then—as is custom with young military couples—got married after less than a year. No, really. We met in March and married in December.

Originally, we'd gotten engaged quickly but planned to have a long engagement. The initial plan was for a wedding in 2004, but for a number of reasons, we decided to move it up to December of 2002.

Given our whirlwind meet-ring-wedding process, it was inevitable that people would suspect a shotgun wedding. At least one close relative looked me right in the eye and asked when I was due. Naturally, being a couple of young, stupid kids, that had to be the reason, right? *Scandalous*.

Well, it wasn't. But once the rings were on, the tune quickly changed from "Oh, you knocked her up, didn't you?" to "When are you two going to have kids?" I almost got whiplash from the sudden shift.

At that point, we were adamant we didn't want kids. At all.

So began the song every childfree person knows by heart: "You'll change your miiiind!"

And... we did.

Eddie was unexpectedly deployed less than a month after we got married. There's usually quite a bit of lead-up to a deployment—sea trials, workups, etc.—and you know it's coming. This time, the ship went out for a three-week training exercise. Ten days into it, he called and said, "We're supposed to be heading home, but I just went outside to take a picture of the sunset... and it's setting off the wrong end of the ship."

This was when the war in Iraq started, and his three weeks at sea would turn out to be eight very long months apart.

And somewhere along the line—somewhere amidst getting through all that separation and wondering when it would be over (we didn't know when he was coming home until a week before he arrived)—we both changed our minds about kids.

That, dear reader, is where this story begins.

PART 2

PLANTING THE SEEDS OF DOUBT

Is this the face of someone who likes her quiet
time interrupted?
(pic by one of my parents, sometime in the 1980s)

CHAPTER 1

FROM CHILDFREE TO INFERTILE

To this day, I can't explain what changed. I can't explain exactly what sent me from adamantly childfree to wanting a baby. For as much as I'd eschewed the idea of being a mother since my early teens, I was suddenly caught up in what some childfree groups refer to as the baby rabies. I really, really wanted to have a baby.

Some people say it must've been the societal expectation. You get married, and then you have kids. We'd checked the first box, so it was time to check the second. I don't know if that was true for us. I really don't. There are any number of explanations for why a person would make this shift, and any number of them *could* have been why I did. When I say I don't know, I mean exactly that. Couldn't explain it then. Won't pretend I can explain it now.

Regardless of which synapse went rogue and why, the fact remained that I now wanted kids. So did Eddie. Our extended separation thanks to the Navy gave us a lot of time to discuss it via phone and email. Were we sure? Did we want to start trying right away or wait a while? How many kids did we want?

Now, at the time, we were not making a lot of money. He was an E4 in the Navy, and even with the housing allowance and separation pay, he wasn't exactly rolling in cash. I was working for a company outside of Seattle that somehow believed ~$13/hour was a decent wage for a supervisor (adjusted for inflation, that's roughly $23/hour). Even back then, the cost of living in that area was eye-watering, and our combined income simply didn't cut it.

I'd say as much in conversations with friends and family, saying I'd love for us to have kids, but I didn't know how we'd afford it.

This was where things got weird. See, I was educated in a very good school district that had comprehensive sex ed, and those classes included everything imaginable to deter us from teen pregnancies. I recall an assignment where we had to go to a store and tally up the prices for a long list of baby necessities (look, this was the 1990s, so no, we couldn't just do it online). We had the rice baby project where we had to carry around a bag of rice representing a baby for a week, and woe be unto anyone whose bag got so much as a scuff. Or anyone who had to carry around a decoy baby for a couple of hours while she waited for someone to bring her the *actual* rice baby she'd left at home that morning. Cough.

Anyway.

We listened at length to how difficult life was with a newborn or toddler, how expensive it was, how enormous of an adjustment it was. You need to wait until you're *stable* and can *afford* that jaw-dropping list of expensive items or it *will* be an unmitigated *disaster*.

So there I was, five years on from my last semester of Ominous Parenthood 101 or whatever it was called. I'm struggling financially. I wanted a baby, but I was comparing prices on generic commissary bread and getting gas at the cheapest places I could find. That list of bottles, wipes, diapers, clothes, pianos, spaceships, and whatever else an infant must have was still there in the back of my mind, its final total blinking red as a voice said, "Lori, this is *way* out of your price range."

As an aside, the jokes I'm making about my school going so hard to prevent teen pregnancy are not a criticism. In fact, given the very low pregnancy rate among my classmates, those classes are effective! I 100% support them—I'm just snarking about the things that still stick with me and made me think twice about having kids as a married adult.

Anyway. I was also working an absurd number of hours on top of a two-hour commute (yes, each way). I had about two hours of downtime each day, and my Saturdays— assuming I wasn't putting in overtime—were for catching up on sleep. I was utterly threadbare when it came to time, sleep, and money.

And yet...

When I talked about this with people around me, there was no grim "Babies are a *lot* of work and a *lot* of money." There was no, "You have your whole life ahead of you—don't throw it all away by having a baby too young."

You see, I had the ring, and that ring apparently unlocked the ability to provide for a child. With that ring on my hand, my concerns were met with, "Nobody's ever ready" and "You *make* it work." People told me, "If everyone waited until they were ready to have kids, no one would ever have any."

Here in 2024, peering back at that era through the lens of a fortysomething, I am more than a little dubious.

Back then, however, in the head of a newlywed twenty-two year-old who wanted a baby that badly, those words were all the green light I needed.

By the time Eddie came back from deployment, we were in agreement: to hell with it, let's have kids.

But... surprise! Turned out that, yet again, everything I'd learned in Scary Biology didn't *quite* match up with reality.

CHAPTER 2

GETTING AN "F" IN APPLIED BIOLOGY

The end of 2003 turned into yet another whirlwind. This would become a theme for us—the military life is not for the faint of heart. While things can happen slowly enough to rival the pace of a lethargic glacier, they can also happen extraordinarily fast.

Eddie returned to Bremerton in September. The original plan had been for him to get out of the Navy when his enlistment ended in December, but after some long conversations, we realized we had two choices:

One, he got out and found a civilian job while I supported us on my ~$13/hour pittance.

Two, he reenlisted, we went wherever the Navy sent us, and I found a job while he supported us on his E4 salary + housing allowance + health insurance.

Kind of a no-brainer at this point.

This was especially true when we factored in that most of the bases where he'd likely end up were in areas with a lower cost of living than Seattle even back then. About 98% of the globe had—and still has—a lower cost of living than Seattle, so odds were pretty good!

Eddie reenlisted at the beginning of December 2003, shortly before our first anniversary, and we were introduced to the concept of slam orders. Normally, when you reenlist or you're up for orders, you're given a list of bases with available billets. You select your top choices in order of preference, and the Navy sends you wherever it wants to anyway. With slam orders, there isn't a list of choices. You get the orders you get, and in our case, we suddenly had less than eight weeks to get to Norfolk, Virginia.

So, off to the East Coast we went. Through all the stress and chaos, the thought of a baby was pretty far in the backs of our minds. As the smoke cleared, though, I realized... my period was late. Like, really late.

Well, damn. That was quick!

But the test was negative. So was the next one. A couple more weeks went by—still no period and still no positive test.

Huh.

I went to a clinic just to get a test, thinking maybe the storebought ones weren't accurate or something. Still negative, and they recommended I see my doctor. Right. That meant I should probably... get a doctor. I'll get into that in the next chapter, because it too is A Story.

What I will say here is that this was my first inkling that infertility was in my future. It turned out that while getting pregnant by accident as a teenager is ridiculously easy, it isn't always that way for adults who *want* to get pregnant.

It wasn't entirely a surprise. Some degree of infertility

runs in my family, with a few years often passing between the wedding and the first baby. Even with that common thread amongst relatives, I'd assumed—as many of us do—that it wouldn't happen to me. After all, I'd spent years in school listening to how often various birth control methods fail and how pregnancy was all but inevitable. Though my teachers didn't say it, it was hard for the teenage ear not to hear, "If you're not doing at least *something* to prevent it, you *will* get pregnant."

I usually got As and Bs in those classes.

But apparently when it came to *applied* biology, I was an "F" student.

And like, I knew infertility was a thing. I wasn't naïve. (Well, I was, but not *that* naïve.) Still, there was something emotionally weird about wrapping my head around "I can't get pregnant." It was like I'd spent all that time hearing how teenagers standing too close together were one strong breeze away from parenthood, but I couldn't do it.

What is wrong with me?

Is this something that can be treated?

Am I ever going to be able to have kids?

Will my husband want to stay with me if I can't?

Even now, sitting happily in my childfree present, I remember vividly how difficult it was to process.

As time wore on—as a few months turned into a year, as a year became plural—it didn't get any easier to process. I became that person who couldn't help but feel sad and frustrated when I saw someone who was pregnant.

Why is it so easy for them?

I started to notice how many people around me had "accidents" and "oops babies." It didn't seem fair. What were they doing that I wasn't? (Ovulating, apparently)

Fortunately, there were options available to suss out what was causing the infertility and—hopefully—treat it. Sign me up!

The thing is, I was so caught up in the frustration and emotion, in wondering what in the world was malfunctioning in my body, that I didn't realize what was coming next.

Not until my struggle slammed me face first into a brick wall of unresolved trauma.

CHAPTER 3

FIRST DO NO HARM

TREATING INFERTILITY AFTER YEARS OF MEDICAL TRAUMA.

One of my earliest and most vivid memories is from when I was maybe three years old. I couldn't begin to tell you why I was at the pediatrician's that day. I can't even remember if it was in his old office or the one he moved his practice to at some point when I was young. What I remember clear as day though is being held down by this doctor and a nurse. I remember horrible pain in my left arm for what seemed like *ages*. And I remember my doctor's somewhat gravelly but familiar and (under normal circumstances) comforting voice soothingly telling me, "It's okay to scream."

They were drawing blood.

I don't remember why. I don't know why they were using a larger needle that day, or even how I know that (someone told me; I just don't recall who or when).

But I remember the pain, and I remember being held down, and I remember hearing, over and over, "It's okay to scream."

I'm forty-three now, and I'm still terrified of hypodermic needles.

When I was in second grade, I needed some small fillings on the sides of my molars. Because there wasn't a lot of drilling required, the decision was made to forego nitrous or Novocain.

The dentist's hand slipped, and the drill went into my gums.

I've never again set foot in a dentist's office without a massive spike of anxiety.

When I was twelve, I had a Plantar wart on the heel of my left foot. It didn't respond to the usual treatment, and in fact got bigger. So, my pediatrician—the same one who did the aforementioned blood draw—decided the best approach was to cut it out. As he took the scalpel from its wrapper, he said, "It's dead tissue, including the nerves, so it won't hurt."

Reader, he was wrong.

Thirty years later, I still won't let anyone touch my feet. I don't even like having things *on* my feet, including socks.

When I was seventeen, I was having serious pain in my jaw, and one side would pop audibly. Every doctor and dentist insisted it was TMJ, because that's what "clicking" indicates. I said, "No, it's not clicking—it's popping." They dismissed that as semantics and continued to address the clicking.

One TMJ specialist was feeling around the joint both inside and outside my mouth, which is about as fun as it sounds. Then he pushed his thumb (which was in my mouth) *into the joint* and *twisted it*. Party and a half, right there. He spoke ominously about the surgery I would need, how my parents' insurance likely wouldn't cover all of it, and how there would be a lengthy and painful recovery.

When I relayed this to another doctor, he referred me to another TMJ specialist. I was dubious of course, and my jaw ached just imagining the joint being manhandled again. This guy was very good, though, and very gentle. He also thought that perhaps in order to get a better idea of what was going on, he should X-ray me with my mouth open instead of closed like all the others.

When the results came back, the reason my jaw was popping—*not clicking*—was because it was completely dislocated on one side.

It had been this way for *two years*, during which time every doctor and dentist dismissed it as TMJ and ignored my insistence it was popping and not clicking. I also had extensive dental work done during this period... with a dislocated jaw. The extensive dental work was a result of my orthodontist ignoring signs of problems in my teeth. And, upon more investigation by my specialist, we figured out that the orthodontist's treatment to correct my overbite had slowly dislocated my jaw.

Twenty-five years later, I still have reduced range of motion, and dental procedures leave my jaw incredibly sore.

These are just a few examples of the medical trauma that has accumulated over the course of my life. I've experienced verbal abuse, neglect, and straight up malpractice, like the time an ER doctor said to me, "We think you may have a spinal cord injury, so we're going to have you walk over to radiology." (No, they weren't kidding, and yes, they made me walk.)

And this doesn't even take into consideration all the fun that comes with being someone with chronic pain. I was diagnosed with fibromyalgia at seventeen, and that was after several years of pain. The same doctor who drew my blood and carved out my heel said I should stop complaining about being in pain all the time because I was stressing my parents out (his words, not theirs), and he dismissed my severe menstrual cramps because "some girls get cramps—it's normal."

All of which is a very long-winded way of saying that when it comes to medical personnel, your girl has some *serious* trust issues.

So there I was in Norfolk in the early months of 2004. The clinic had confirmed I was not pregnant, and they'd told me I needed to see an OB/Gyn to figure out what was going on.

We were new to the city and still settling in, so we hadn't even found a primary care doctor yet. Being Norfolk, there were a lot of military medical facilities, but I balked. Spending my formative years on the periphery of military life, I'd heard as many horror stories about military medical as I'd heard sea stories. If you've been around the military in any capacity, you know they tell *a lot* of sea stories (or whatever the equivalent is for the land-based branches). Needless to say, between those stories and my own trauma, I was leery of going to a military facility.

I found a civilian OB/Gyn and made an appointment.

As was normal for me, I was nervous on the way in. I spent the time in the waiting room reminding myself that just because I'd had some bad experiences—okay, a lot of bad experiences—didn't mean I'd have one now. There were plenty of good doctors out there. I was bound to find one eventually. Right?

The doctor was snippy and terse. When he went to do an exam, I was—surprise, surprise—a little tense. It didn't help that the speculum he was using was a) metal and b) cold.

No problem, according to the doctor. Did he give me a chance to relax? Did he warm up the speculum?

Nope. He leaned on that sucker and *made* it go in.

If you just crossed your legs and winced, you're in good company, because I did the same thing while I was writing that. In fact, the nurse who was in the room—since they were required to have a woman present with the male doctor—winced and *looked away*. She didn't say a word. Her face said it all as he did his exam, but she didn't say or do anything except flinch away whenever he was rough.

After that was over, he told me to get dressed and come into his office. There, he explained to me that there was nothing wrong with my system, and that my periods had stopped because I was fat. (To be clear, I was probably 20 lbs. overweight at that point; not ideal, but not exactly catastrophic.)

"Lose ten pounds," he declared, "and your periods will come back."

I tried to argue that my weight hadn't changed recently, but my periods had, so that didn't seem right.

He dismissed the idea and said, "You don't want to start out fat anyway because you're going to gain weight when you're pregnant."

That night was the first time my husband ever saw me cry. I was also in a ton of pain and bleeding, and I worried I should go to the emergency room. I hesitated, though, because I knew they'd do a pelvic exam. They'd have to in order to see if there was any damage. After everything Dr. Satan had done to put me in that much pain, the thought of having an exam made me literally sick to my stomach.

After two days, the pain wasn't any better and there was still some bleeding, so I finally went in. I pleaded with them for a female doctor because, rational or not, I was terrified of having a man give me an exam. Unfortunately, there wasn't a woman available, but the man who was assigned to me was very kind and very gentle. He found some bruising and tearing, but it was nothing serious; it would heal on its own. (Also, this was a military hospital, so the horror stories weren't *all* true.)

So now I found myself going into this infertility struggle with not only everything I'd already been through, but some fresh trauma. Our infertility journey would last for four years, and every single time I had to have any kind of exam, I went back to that day with Dr. Satan. About twenty years later, I still do. He's long since retired now, and I hope his butthole is permanently itchy.

The one silver lining to the experience with him was that I found a voice I'd never had before. I found my backbone. From then on, every single doctor or nurse who was going to touch me in that area heard what happened with him. Before they laid a finger on me, I needed them to understand where my anxiety was coming from. If they made excuses for him, if they didn't take me seriously, or if they cut me off, I fired them. Plain and simple.

Even now, twenty years later, I do the same thing with new doctors. If they don't have time to let me explain that I have legitimate trauma associated with pelvic exams, then they don't need my money. Every time I go to a new OB/Gyn or general practitioner, we have a conversation about it, and we do it while I'm still dressed.

What really sucks is that pelvic exams were one of the few areas where I *didn't* have a lot of anxiety. The first time I had one was with a nurse practitioner who was respectful, compassionate, and very easygoing. She'd explain what she was doing but also talk about other things to help me relax. She even taped pictures to the ceiling so patients had something to focus on. Eighteen-year-old me walked out afterward thinking, "Huh. That was easy," and I never had any issues with my annual appointments.

Right up until one asshole with a metal speculum took that away from me.

The awful experience with him and my pile of past trauma didn't scare me away from having a baby, but I'd be lying if I said they didn't make the prospect of fertility treatments, pregnancy, and childbirth a whole lot scarier.

I'd also be lying if I said that experience was the last negative one I'd have during this process.

Not long after I crossed paths with Dr. Satan, a friend suggested her OB/Gyn, saying she was very good and would definitely listen.

At first, I liked her. She listened to me, and she thought Dr. Satan's assessment of my weight as the culprit was nonsense.

"I have patients who are much bigger than you," she said, "who have no problem at all getting pregnant. I also have patients who are smaller and struggle. Simply being over-weight isn't a cause of infertility."

She did some exams and tests, and she ultimately concluded that there was nothing "wrong," per se. No under-lying diseases. No structural problems. No hormonal wonki-ness. In her words, "Some people don't ovulate regularly, and we don't really know why." Her solution? Put me on Provera, a hormone that would stimulate ovulation.

Forty-three year-old me would very much like to go back in time and cuff twenty-three year-old me upside the head. I was still so trusting back then. So willing to accept that I was hearing the truth. In my defense, my problematic doctors had usually shown their true colors pretty quickly. I had, I believed, learned the signs of someone who didn't have my best interest in mind or didn't care enough to give me all the information. I was not as compelled as I am now to go home and research the bejeezus out of anything and everything they said.

So when I asked about side effects, I took her at her word when she said, "Some people experience a little bloating."

Fast forward about seventy-two hours.

I was three days into a ten-day prescription, and I was in hell. Every joint in my body ached. I couldn't concentrate. I was fighting so hard not to let the mood swings show that I finally broke down crying in the middle of the freeway on the way home from work (and anyone who knows me will tell you that I'm not one to cry over much of anything). I couldn't sleep, and when I did, I had horrible nightmares. I could. Not. *Function*.

In a panic, I called my doctor's office on the morning of day four. No one answered, so I left a message. I said I was on Provera and the side effects were overwhelming, and I needed to talk to someone *today*. It couldn't wait. I pleaded for someone to call me ASAP and emphasized that I *needed* a call back *today*.

No one called.

I frantically searched online to see if it was safe to just stop taking the pills. Everything warned ominously not to stop without consulting your doctor, but... my doctor wouldn't call me back. No one from the office would.

The next day, I called again and again until I got a person, and when I finally did, I asked why no one had called.

"You said you were going on vacation," came the response.

I replied that I most certainly had not. "I said I needed someone to call me back right away because it was urgent, not because I was going on vacation."

From there, I tried to make an appointment, but there was nothing available. I pleaded with them to have my doctor or a nurse call me. I was an absolute mess, physically and mentally, and I needed *someone* to tell me what to do next.

A nurse finally called me to relay the message that I could stop taking the Provera if I needed to. I pushed to make an appointment so I could talk to my doctor, but the nurse kept insisting that the effects would abate after I stopped the meds.

I understood that doctors are often too busy to come to the phone, but at this point, I was very much getting the impression everyone there was trying to brush me off. I thought that might be the drugs talking—hormones *suck*—so I ran the story by a friend, and she agreed that it didn't sound right.

I decided I wasn't comfortable proceeding with this doctor. Maybe I was being too sensitive, but quite frankly, on the heels of my run-in with Dr. Satan, I was done giving the benefit of the doubt when I felt I wasn't being treated appropriately.

That appointment where I was given the Provera prescription? That turned out to be the last time I spoke to that doctor until almost a year later. In fact, I didn't seek any treatment for several months after that, hoping nature would just take its course and the problem would resolve itself.

In early 2005, I had a miscarriage. I didn't even know I was pregnant until that point, so emotionally, it wasn't as devastating as I expected. It was also very, very early (maybe 5 weeks?), so while it wasn't fun, it wasn't terrible either.

Not long after that, the doctor's office sent me a reminder that it was time for my annual exam. I wasn't keen on seeing her again, but some time and distance had cooled the anger, and I decided to give her another chance.

She was dismissive about the incident with Provera, saying we'd just have to find a different solution, but not really apologizing or even acknowledging anything else. She shrugged off my comments that the side effects were in line with Provera's known side effects, and that all I'd really been asking for was a phone call.

I'd already decided at this point that I wasn't going to see her again after this. I'd let her do the PAP just to get it done, since at least I knew she could be trusted with that, which gave her one up on a stranger. Then I was done.

As she ran me through the usual pre-exam questions, I mentioned that I'd had an early miscarriage a couple of months prior. She asked if I'd gone to the ER or had a D&C, since I hadn't contacted her office.

I said I had not. It happened on its own, was mostly over by the time I realized what it was, and there really wasn't any reason to see anyone about it. (Especially when that would mean a pelvic exam, and we all know how I feel about those.)

She *yelled at me.* "What do you mean, you didn't go see anyone? You could've had an infection! Retained tissue!"

I was taken aback—I also have some delightful trauma responses to people shouting at me—but I managed to explain that I'd read up on what symptoms to watch for, and I hadn't seen anything indicative that I needed medical attention.

She wasn't pleased by that, and she let me know it. When she'd finally run out of steam, she huffed and said, "Well, at least now we know you *can* get pregnant."

Silver linings and all that, I guess.

After that, I was 100% done with her. I didn't want her to touch me. But it turns out my recently discovered backbone withers beneath the weight of the trauma response that comes after someone shouts at me.

I won't say her exam was worse than the one Dr. Satan did, but it wasn't fun.

Afterward, I left her office and never darkened its doorway again.

I also realized that between her and Dr. Satan, I couldn't

keep doing this. The trust was gone. I wanted to do something about my infertility, but just the thought of seeing another OB/Gyn made me physically ill.

So, at a loss for what else to do, I started looking into alternatives.

CHAPTER 4

THIS CAN'T BE THE ONLY WAY
SEEKING ALTERNATIVE CARE

This chapter is probably going to ruffle some feathers, so I want to make a few things crystal clear up front.

- None of this is medical advice.
- None of it is advice at all—it's my experience and nothing more.
- I am not a healthcare provider of any kind. Again, this is all my experience and nothing more.
- We're on the same page here, right? Medical advice—no. Personal experience—yes.

With all of that out of the way, I decided to start looking outside of modern Western medicine in search of some kind of alternative. At the recommendation of a friend, I decided to try a midwife and see if she had any thoughts or insights that I hadn't found with my doctors.

That was certainly an eye-opening and game-changing visit. My midwife, Beth, rejected my doctor's assertion that "some women don't ovulate and we don't know why," along with Dr. Satan's declaration that everything was a result of me being fat. She actually laughed at what Dr. Satan had said, since she was quite a bit heavier than me, was pregnant with her tenth child, and had clients of all sizes who'd suffered from infertility.

As we went through my medical history, she had some theories, and she recommended some various tests that no one had suggested before. At this point, I was in my mid-twenties, so I'd been having periods for about ten years. Horrifically painful, seriously heavy, and wildly irregular periods. For ten years. The same doctor who told me that "some girls get cramps" also said, "The pill will help."

That was the extent of any attempts to figure out why I had so much pain. It was just one of those things, and here, this pill will help. End of conversation.

Beth was the *first* to suggest there might be an underlying issue—one that was causing both my infertility *and* my miserable periods.

And that's the story of how I eventually found out—in my mid-twenties and knee-deep in infertility—that I had polycystic ovarian syndrome (PCOS) *and* endometriosis.

Fan. *Tastic.*

So now we had some idea what was causing the infertility.

This was where things got a little weird. I wasn't at all surprised that there wasn't much a midwife could do. What I didn't expect was for her to recommend a chiropractor and... an acupuncturist? Really?

But you know what? After all the BS leading up to this point, I'd have gone to the circus if someone said it might help.

The chiropractor didn't last long. He had a really strange setup with two tables out in the open where he and his partner would adjust people. They ran us through like an assembly line, adjusting us right in front of all the other waiting patients while both chiropractors spoke at length—to everyone in the room—about the benefits of chiropractic medicine. It was almost like listening to the son of a preacher and a used car salesman, all while having my neck and back cracked in front of strangers.

I know this isn't how most chiropractors operate, but it still left a bad taste in my mouth. It was particularly off-putting when I explained that I wanted them to stop cracking my neck. I've had some neck injuries in the past, and I also have a phobia about things around or people messing with my neck (I'm not sure why, only that it is an incredibly deep fear). Having my head cranked to the left and right until my spine cracked was—well, it still makes me shudder just thinking about it. When it became clear they weren't interested in leaving my neck alone, and that their entire "treatment" was giving everyone the same adjustment in between spouting their sales pitches, I decided I was done.

So the chiropractic route didn't work out. I couldn't bring myself to try it again because even now, just thinking about it makes my skin crawl at the memory of feeling like my neck was going to snap. *No*, thank you.

Beth had also recommended acupuncture.

That... did not sound appealing to me at all. Remember what I said about being traumatized by a needle when I was a kid? Yeah, acupuncture sounded *fantastic*.

But I'd been burned by doctors and now a chiropractor. The third time was going to be the charm one way or another —either it was going to work miraculously, or it was going to be a disaster. At this point, I didn't even know which option I was betting on, but I made the call to John, the acupuncturist Beth recommended. (Who am I kidding? I'm a Millennial—I don't call people. I sent him an email.)

The first surprise was that the needles aren't bad. They sting briefly, but by the time the pain has registered, it's already gone. Sometimes the muscle aches after the sting has gone away. There was one in my shin that made my whole calf ache. Some of the ones in my hands were really achy. Not fun, but not bad.

The really weird part was that...

It worked.

Like... it really, really worked.

I have a lot of feelings about acupuncture. It actually *annoys* me that it works as well as it does. It *shouldn't* do what it does, damn it!

But I couldn't—and still can't—argue with the results.

After a few appointments, he'd recommended a partic-ular supplement. I usually had my appointments before work, but I didn't have one that day. Instead, I figured I'd just swing in and pick up the supplement, then continue to work. Nothing out of the ordinary.

As I pulled into his parking lot, I had already decided I

was calling in sick to work. I'd felt a bit meh when I left home because my period had started, but in the half hour it took me to drive to his clinic, the cramps had come in with a *vengeance*. I could barely stand.

What I needed to do was call in sick, drive my butt home, take more than the recommended dose of Midol, and spend the rest of the day begging for sweet death. (Don't judge me—cramps hurt!)

I was already there, though, so I went inside. Might as well at least get my supplements, *then* go home and beg for sweet death.

As his receptionist and I were settling up the bill, John came into the waiting area. He took one look at me and knew something was off. Not that it took much power of observation to figure that out—I was hunched over the desk and probably looked like I was about to get sick. I sure felt the part.

"I got you, fam," he said. Well, not quite. It was more professional than that, but you get the idea. He disappeared into the back, and when he reemerged, he held up a tiny square of what looked like an adhesive bandage—as if someone had cut off a piece of a Band-Aid about half an inch square. In the center was something that resembled a large grain of sand or maybe a sesame seed. It was a seed of some sort, but don't ask me to tell you what kind.

Then he told me to brush my hair back so he could... put it in my ear? What?

I was in a ton of pain, though, so I didn't argue. I brushed my hair back, and he carefully pressed the seed just inside the cartilage of my ear. It kind of hurt, a little like a rock in my shoe, but it wasn't bad. Then he used the adhesive to keep it there.

"Press on it," he told me.

I did.

And the whole world shifted. I wasn't dizzy like I was blacking out—more like the room was spinning. It was seriously intense and weird.

Fortunately, it only lasted a couple of seconds, and when it stopped...

"What the hell?" I asked John. "It doesn't hurt anymore!"

He just gave me a knowing little smile and told me that if the cramps started up again, push on the seed.

I didn't call in sick to work after all, and you better believe I kept that thing in my ear for the rest of the day. To this day, years later, I will still dig my fingernail into that spot when my cramps get too intense, and it still works wonders.

That was one incident that really sticks out in my mind, but my time as John's patient was peppered with a lot of similar moments. Usually moments when I realized something he did had some kind of effect it really shouldn't have. Like when the needles in my shoulder eased some of the pain and inflammation from an old injury that liked to flare up sometimes. Or when, after a few weeks of being treated three times a week, my periods became more regular and a lot less painful.

Another odd part about acupuncture is that it involves putting needles in the feet. Various parts of the feet correspond with parts of the body. The ear, too—I ended up with a lot of needles in my ears. But remember how I mentioned earlier that I don't let anyone touch my feet after my pediatrician cut into my heel with a scalpel? Yeah. That made acupuncture complicated.

John was good at what he did, though, and unlike the long parade of doctors and nurses before him, he respected my boundaries. He only touched my feet long enough to insert and remove needles. He was careful about how he touched them—firmly, so it wasn't ticklish, and only for as long as absolutely necessary. Within a few months, he could touch them without any preamble or extra caution. This man was able to work past *two* of my oldest and deepest medical traumas at the same time without freaking me out, pushing my boundaries, or ever making me uncomfortable. That's not an endorsement of acupuncture, but it should very firmly illustrate the level of respect and trust he was able to cultivate when other providers didn't bother.

Probably the most bizarre thing (besides the seed in my ear making my cramps go away) came about six months after I started seeing him. We were talking during an appointment, and I commented, "I've been dealing with chronic pain and fibromyalgia symptoms for years, but I swear, it's all been gone for the last couple of months."

"Of course it has," he said, admittedly a little smugly. "You don't have it anymore."

It didn't seem that simple, but I mean... the symptoms *were* gone. And they stayed gone. After years and years of getting absolutely nowhere with any kind of treatment, I wasn't in pain anymore.

I want to make it clear here that I'm not trying to sell acupuncture to anyone. It's not a magic cure-all. Like I said in the beginning, it actually annoys me sometimes that it works because it just doesn't make sense and it *shouldn't* work.

It's also not something I would use to replace Western medicine for something like cancer or a condition requiring surgery. In fact, when I lived in Nebraska years later, I had an acupuncturist who worked closely with my orthopedist as well as my personal trainer after I reinjured my shoulder. That acupuncturist had a few patients who were seeing him to relieve chemotherapy-related nausea; they were still getting conventional cancer treatment, but under the guidance of their doctors, were also getting help with symptoms and side effects via acupuncture. So, even with my trust issues relating to *practitioners* of Western medicine, I don't eschew it or avoid it. Acupuncture works for some things, Western medicine works for others, and they aren't mutually exclusive.

What I do know is that despite my skepticism and despite my inability to explain how it works, I felt better in a lot of ways after John started treating me. Some of the improvements continued for *years* after I moved away. To this day, my periods are still more regular and less violent than they were from my teens into my twenties, even with perimenopause beginning to wreak havoc. My shoulder was less prone to flaring up until I reinjured it in 2014.

The fibromyalgia—I don't know, man. I really don't. Maybe it was something else? Maybe I was misdiagnosed? It's impossible to say. But whatever it was, it's gone. It's *still* gone. When I started seeing the other acupuncturist in 2012—four years after the last time I saw John—I still didn't have any fibro symptoms, and I don't have any today. When I've injured myself since, I don't get that ripple effect of full-body pain, and even now in my forties, I recover from injuries like a person without fibro.

Yeah, I don't know either. I just don't argue with it.

Anyway, back to 2005 or so when I started seeing John, I was there to iron out these stupid fertility issues. He put me on some various supplements—I couldn't begin to recall what they were or what they did—and had me in his office two or three times a week for acupuncture treatment.

He had me make some dietary changes that made an enormous difference. For one thing, thanks to my incredibly heavy periods—the ones my doctors weren't at all concerned about—I'd been anemic or borderline anemic since I was fourteen. Doctors had put me on iron supplements a few times, but they did absolutely nothing. They'd given me lists of vegetables to eat to increase my iron levels, but the changes were negligible.

John recommended at least one serving of red meat every day for two weeks. After that, my iron levels tested normal for the first time in over a decade. The conclusion was that for whatever reason, my body doesn't absorb enough iron from supplements or from most foods, but it will absorb it from meat. Of course he didn't recommend having a steak every night for the rest of my life. What he did recommend was eating red meat during and after my period, and any time I started feeling anemic. From then on, even now almost twenty years later, my iron levels have consistently remained normal or on the lower end of normal.

I felt better than I had in years. Far less pain. Far less of the fatigue and lightheadedness that always signaled my iron levels were down. I didn't have to call in sick to work because of cramps anymore. Even my migraines started to get a lot better. Getting pregnant still wasn't happening, but my body was functioning better, which was promising.

To this day, I still don't understand how or why the acupuncture or anything else he did worked.

But after everything I'd been through to get to this point, I wasn't looking a gift horse in the mouth.

CHAPTER 5

BOOKS, BOARDS, & BS

LEARNING JUST HOW ILL-EQUIPPED I AM TO BECOME
A MOTHER.

I am very much the kind of person who will research every-thing into the ground, especially when it comes to my health. I don't believe I have an M.D. bestowed upon me by Google University, but I have learned the hard way that I need to arm myself with as much information as possible in order to advo-cate for myself. Trust issues will do that to you.

It's served me well, too. Story time!

In 2018, I was diagnosed with Idiopathic Intracranial Hypertension. It's quite rare, and not a lot of doctors know much about it. We were stationed in Spain at the time, and I needed to see a neurologist, which the base didn't have. So, I needed a referral to a Spanish neurologist, and the referral had to come from my primary care doctor, not the optometrist who'd diagnosed me. At this point, I hadn't even *met* my PCM yet, but whatever—I needed to see the neurologist. So... fine.

The doctor admitted right off the bat that he'd never even

heard of IIH and had no idea what it was or what I needed. He signed off on the referral because he took the optometrist at his word that I needed to go. Later, the neurologist prescribed a medication to help with the IIH, but he also wanted me to have an MRI. I needed to have a referral for that, too, so it was back to the PCM.

During this appointment, I brought up the fact that IIH is most common in overweight women of childbearing age, and that a lot of doctors push for weight loss as a solution. I mostly mentioned this to explain why I had actually gone through two neurologists at this point; I'd summarily fired the first one after she said she didn't believe PCOS was a legitimate hinderance to weight loss because, quote, "Well, then apparently no one had PCOS in concentration camps."

No, I am not making that up.

Anyway, my PCM commented that since I do have PCOS and therefore struggle to lose weight, there was a medication available that could help. It was meant for diabetics, but it also showed great results in helping people like me. It helps with insulin resistance, which is a common problem associated with PCOS. I asked if it was safe to take it with the medication I was currently taking, and he assured me it was absolutely fine.

My gut said... *Are you sure about that, Commander? Because last time we talked, you knew nothing about my condition or my medication.*

After I picked up my prescriptions, I went home, and I immediately looked up both medications and whether they had any negative interactions.

Lo and behold, it's well-documented that taking these two drugs together meant a significant risk of *kidney failure*.

Like I said... trust issues.

And the reason I'm telling this story is to illustrate how I'm not claiming to be smarter than my doctors, or that I'm on the same level as an M.D. I just have to be my own advocate, and that means second-guessing *everything*. It means being aware that doctors are not infallible, that they don't know everything, and that they can't be expected to know every single drug interaction or what have you off the top of their head. The problem was that he didn't respond, "I don't know —let me check." He confidently told me the drugs could be taken together without issue.

This incident was, of course, many years after the point in my story where this chapter began, but it was the best anecdote to illustrate how I've learned to advocate for myself because no one else will, and why I *still* have to do so.

Back in 2006-2007, as our infertility journey was unfolding, I was less confident in asserting myself and advocating for myself, but I wasn't a complete doormat. I was already deeply in the habit of researching, researching, researching, both to make sure I was getting the full story and just to understand what was happening, if I had other options, etc.

I had a feeling this situation wasn't going to resolve itself any time soon, so I decided it was as good a time as any to start researching and learning as much as I could. Now, when I research things, I deep dive. I want to know everything, and I read whatever I can get my hands on—the good, the bad, and the ugly.

I'll listen to people share their experiences. I'll read peer-reviewed studies. Reality, it seems, is often tucked in between those two—the data shows that the individual experience is the exception, not the rule, and the individual experience cautions that the data can't possibly account for every situation and variable.

In the realms of pregnancy, childbirth, and parenthood, there was far more controversy and conflict than I'd imagined, often with research and experiences firmly backing up *both* sides. This is also one of those realms where everyone *Knows Everything*, and people will often dismiss other experiences or even data that doesn't line up with their lived experience. When you're trying to suss out the truth and get a bead on what your future experience might look like, the water gets incredibly muddy.

Doing that no-holds-barred deep dive into an area full of contradiction and controversy when you have a lifetime of medical trauma?

That was... an experience.

It was difficult to be objective, too. For example, there was a ton of debate on some message boards about C-sections. Some people argued that a planned C-section was safer than a natural birth. Others posited that the procedure was overused and even that surgeons prioritized convenience over safety. There were myriad other discussions of every imaginable pro and con, including countless that I hadn't even thought of, and those discussions could get seriously heated. Plus there were people recounting their experiences, which ran the gamut from great to tragic.

And then there was me, filtering it all through a lens of

medical trauma and a deep distrust of medical professionals. That was fun.

I also spent a lot of time reading birth stories ranging from super easy to horrific. I wanted to know every way things could go, for better or worse, because I don't like being blind-sided. I'm generally pretty good at being objective about things and reminding myself that a worst-case scenario isn't the norm, but as with the discussions mentioned previously, there was that pesky lens of bad experiences.

This only got worse as certain themes kept popping up over and over and over again:

"The pain relief wasn't working, but no one would listen."

"I reiterated that I'm allergic to X, but no one would listen."

"I knew something was wrong, but no one would listen."

For someone with my background, that constant drumbeat of "no one would listen" was straight up terrifying. It made me dig deeper, searching for answers and reassurance. I wanted the bald truth, but I also wanted to know it was going to be okay.

Except... it wasn't always okay. Not everyone survived. Not everyone thrived. People were left traumatized, only to have that trauma dismissed because "You have a healthy baby —that's all that matters."

Uh, no. That *isn't* all that matters. The mother is still a whole person with thoughts and feelings, and I encountered an alarming number who'd been through utter hell en route to motherhood. Horribly complicated pregnancies. Terrifying births. Some described what was nothing short of battery at the hands of medical professionals, and as someone who *still* can't go to an OB/Gyn without having a trauma response, my growing fears in this department were a lot more complicated than just, "Wow, this is gonna hurt."

So if I did get pregnant, who did I trust to help me through to the other end? The medical professionals I'd been conditioned to distrust? My own body, which didn't exactly have the greatest track record of functioning properly?

In addition to talking to my most recent providers, who I did trust so far, I did more research. I did a ton of reading across a broad spectrum, from books written by midwives to those written by doctors and nurses. I found books by parents about their experiences, which was eye-opening for someone this clueless about babies and kids. I even picked up a few textbooks and read peer-reviewed papers online. Anything I could get my hands on, I devoured.

I also, as I alluded to above, joined the infamous online mommy boards. That was where I found even *more* tales of birth trauma, complications, and a whole cornucopia of reasons why the whole process of reproduction was sounding less and less appealing.

There were a lot of *good* stories, though, and I made sure to read as many of those as I could find, too. I didn't want to go into this in a panic—I just wanted to be informed, ideally with as much balance as I could manage. The fears associated with facing down my medical trauma weren't going to scare me away from having a baby, but they were real, and they were something I was trying to deal with the best way I knew how. I've often heard fear described as a gift—it's that sense that makes us take notice of our surroundings and take threats seriously. In this case, it was what drove me to try to understand as much as possible so that I could do everything within my power to minimize risks, or at the very least, be aware of them.

The boards I joined covered an incredibly broad spectrum of topics. There were everything from "year" groups—so, people whose kids were born in a specific year or even month—to boards where people held debates. There were support groups for pregnancy loss, people with special needs kids, military families, divorced parents, widowed parents, stepparents—it really ran the gamut of any imaginable niche for parents supporting other parents.

For someone like me, it was a great place to just quietly observe and learn. It was incredibly educational on a lot of fronts.

What I learned about the most? Myself, even if some of what I learned didn't fully crystallize until I looked back on it years later.

For one thing, whenever I visited these boards, I gravitated toward the debate boards. Not just those relating to parenthood—breastfeeding vs. formula, circumcision, etc.—but religion, political topics, and social issues. I spent time on the support boards for everything from fertility issues to dealing with school-age children and older, but it was the debate boards that held my interest more than anything. When the pandemic hit many years later, I was already a seasoned veteran of the vaccine debate thanks to those boards.

In retrospect, that should've been a big, fat clue, especially the part where I felt wildly out of place on any boards *except* the debate boards. It was a little like imposter syndrome, which I still get today even after fifteen years as an author, except I didn't feel like a novice writer among experienced pros. I felt like I just... didn't belong there. I didn't vibe with these people. There was a profound disconnect that I didn't know how to bridge. Reading people's stories or listening to them talk about their experiences with children (or the experiences they were looking forward to) only widened that chasm between them and me.

For example, I've trained horses, and I always got excited when we had a breakthrough and they learned something new. But the prospect of teaching a kid something or watching them learn how to do things just didn't evoke much reaction. I saw a lot of prospective parents who were eager to teach things to their future kids, but that didn't register with me. Not the way it seemed like it should have.

I enjoy taking people places they've never been and watching them experience something for the first time... as adults. I love going to things like theme parks, touristy spots, eccentric and silly stores, zoos, art museums, shows... as an adult. With other adults. On adult terms. I like being able to tap out when the crowds get overwhelming or the day gets too hot. I like being relaxed and knowing that if I get separated from the people I'm with, they can take care of themselves until we find each other again. The thought of going to these places and events with children doesn't make me excited at the prospect of experiencing it with them—it just makes me not want to go at all.

I kept reminding myself that was all because I'd never

done those things with *my* child. It would be different when they were mine, and I was just overthinking it.

But I'd be lying if I said it didn't stick in the back of my mind.

One positive aspect of the mommy boards was that I learned how to debate. I gained a lot of new insight about things I'd never considered; the political commentary I sometimes do on social media now is largely influenced by that experience. So even though I ultimately decided not to become a mother myself, I won't say the time I spent on those forums was wasted.

Another reason I started reading books and visiting message boards was that—quite frankly—I had very little experience with young children except when I was still one of their peers. When it came to interacting with them as an adult, I was clueless. Still am, if I'm honest.

It didn't help that I wasn't around a lot of little kids growing up. I was on the older end of my classmates in school (the cutoff for each grade is the beginning of September and my birthday is in October), but outside of school, I was nearly always one of the youngest—if not *the* youngest—in social groups. My house was one of four in a small cluster in our neighborhood, and each house had two kids who did a lot of growing up together. I was the second youngest of those eight kids, and I only had two years on the youngest.

I was also the younger of two siblings, the youngest of most of my cousins for many years—I have *second* cousins who are older than me—and the youngest in a lot of my social circles. On the rare occasion when I babysat as a teenager, it was usually for kids who were a little older—past the nonambulatory and diaper stages—so it wasn't so bad. Plus, I wasn't parenting in those situations. All I had to do was keep them alive, out of trouble, fed, and reasonably entertained until their parents came home or they went to bed, whichever came first.

So, by the time I got into my twenties and wanted kids, I was painfully aware of how little I knew about them and how clueless I was about interacting with them. But still, it shouldn't have been *this* alien. I shouldn't have been *that* disconnected from children.

Maybe what I needed more than anything was to learn from people in real-time. Observe the parents and families in my orbit. Listen more closely to friends, coworkers, and family members when they talked about their kids and their experiences as parents. Find out what really makes all these parents tick.

Maybe then I'd figure out exactly where the disconnect was.

CHAPTER 6

PLANTING THE SEEDS OF DOUBT:

HOW PARENTS HELPED TALK ME OUT OF HAVING KIDS

When people discuss being childfree, especially on ye olde internet, a common misconception is that it's childfree people convincing other people to be childfree. It's just angry, hateful, future cat owners wooing would-be parents over to the Dark Side with promises of a carefree drunken life.

It's not, of course, but what a lot of people also don't realize is how much parents contribute to decisions to be childfree. This doesn't apply to all parents or all childfree people, but it does happen.

Sometimes it's parents straight up warning people not to have kids. Believe it or not, it absolutely happens. Usually when there's no one else within earshot or they're safely hidden behind a throwaway account and a VPN, but yes, it happens. There's a lot more *"I love my kids but hate being a parent"* on the internet than people realize.

Other times, they just make comments about their lives as parents, and those of us who don't have kids absorb those comments. For me, it did evoke some empathy and sympathy —because let's be real, some of it sounds incredibly miserable —but it also started to erode my desire to have children. The more I listened, the more I recognized patterns, and the more I wondered... "*Do* I want this? *Is* that the life I want?"

I'll get to the seeds of doubt planted by parents in a minute. First, there were some doubts creeping in on their own based on my own thoughts and observations. In listening to or watching other peoples' experiences, not to mention thinking back to studying developmental psychology in college, some uncomfortable truths about myself started to emerge.

Children go through various developmental stages, and those stages bring with them certain behaviors that are perfectly normal and expected. Tantrums. Sibling rivalry. Defiance. The messiness and clumsiness that come with honing fine motor skills. Being loud. Crying. Waking up throughout the night. It's all part of being a kid, and there's nothing wrong with any of it.

But I was starting to realize that... I don't want to deal with those things. They're perfectly age-appropriate, and the kids aren't doing anything "wrong" per se, but if I'm being fully and brutally honest with myself—I *can't* handle them. And even if I can, I don't want to. I can handle a lot of things, but that doesn't mean I'm inclined to sign up for them unless the payoff is worthwhile.

Of course it's worthwhile. You'll never know love until you have a kid, right? You'll get through eighteen years of struggle, and then you'll have someone to visit you and take care of you when you're old.

In the grand scheme of things, eighteen years isn't a long time.

But... it's also a long time. It's a long time to volunteer for things you can barely imagine tolerating for a single night or a weekend of babysitting. I can barely handle being on the same plane as a baby who is (understandably!) crying from the pressure changes; am I being realistic in thinking I'd want to be the parent trying to comfort them?

Whenever non-parents mention this—whether they're childfree or they're planning to have kids at some point—it's immediately dismissed as "Oh, it's different when they're yours" or "Oh, you'll get used to it." If nothing else, "It's only a few years and it's over before you know it."

"Those behaviors drive you nuts when it's other *people's* kids," we're told. "When they're your own, you don't even really hear the crying and screaming anymore."

That line of thinking never sat quite right with me.

Maybe I'm dubious because I knew parents during my youth who clearly *didn't* have a sudden shift once the kid was theirs. Some expected their kids to just... not do those age-appropriate behaviors that they found irritating. Others punished them for it or otherwise made things worse for themselves and the kid. But it didn't seem like anybody involved was enjoying much of anything.

I also saw and still see parents (especially moms) buckle under it all. Sometimes they'll vent on social media. Sometimes a glass of wine or two out of their kids' earshot will bring out the tearful admissions of, "I don't know how much more I can take" and "It's just so *frustrating*."

And like, we all hit breaking points, even with things we

love. I have never been happier than I am in the career I have now, and the worst day as a writer still beats the best day in customer service (okay, that's a low bar, but stick with me). Still, I occasionally have days where the pressure of meeting a deadline gets to me, or when a book just refuses to come together, and the frustration becomes too much. It's life. Ups and downs happen.

So it's perfectly understandable for parents who love being parents to have moments where it's just too much and they need a break. It doesn't mean they shouldn't be parents or that they made a mistake.

But for me, I was beginning to wonder if I really wanted to sign up for this. Kids are a package deal. Did I really want to opt in to years of behaviors that were normal for a kid but nails on a chalkboard for me? How much faith was I really going to put into "it's different when they're your own"? Because if it turned out I still couldn't handle those behaviors, it wasn't like I could send the kid back for a refund.

That was something I was also starting to question as I watched and listened to parents: *Is* it really different when they're your own? Or is it because you don't have a choice? When there's absolutely no escape and no alternative, we'll all tolerate a lot that we didn't think we could.

It reminds me a little of conversations between those with chronic pain and those without. Those without often say things like, "I couldn't live like that" or "How do you handle being in pain all the time?" And the response is basically, "Because I don't have a choice." When you're in constant pain, it doesn't stop hurting just because it's your new normal. Does your tolerance increase? Absolutely. Do you ever just become numb to it or learn to like it? *No.* You just keep moving forward because what else can you do?

And no, I'm not comparing a baby to chronic pain. Rather, I'm comparing the idea of being in a situation that you can't escape or change. You don't magically start enjoying sleepless nights and restaurant tantrums because it's your own kid; you just learn to address it and cope with it as best you can because what else can you do?

It's an imperfect analogy, of course, but where my mind went here is that I wasn't so sure I wanted to sign up for a life that I had to learn to tolerate or knuckle through.

But, I told myself again and again, people love their kids. People love being parents. Why would it be so different for me? I knew plenty of parents who had been indifferent about kids—or even outright disliked kids—but clearly loved their own.

So I'd be fine, wouldn't I?

Except then I started really listening to parents. Not just passively listening, but *asking*. Especially during the latter half of our infertility struggle, I started asking parents to be straight with me. I wanted them to answer me bluntly and honestly.

"I want to go into this with my eyes open," I told them. "Don't sugarcoat it."

Reader, they did not sugarcoat it.

For example, when I asked about sleep deprivation and being tired:

> "You're never *not* tired. Ever. You will learn a whole
> new dimension of tired."

I'd heard that a lot. In fact, I found myself getting incredibly annoyed with parents because whenever I made a comment about being tired or not getting enough sleep, a parent would laugh and tell me I didn't know what tired was. That was aggravating because I've been an insomniac my whole life and, quite frankly, it's not a competition.

But it also added to that rapidly growing pile of doubts. *Was* this really what I wanted?

Someone once told me that night owls working on day schedules live in a perpetual state of jetlag because their circadian rhythms never line up with their lives. This was very true for me. One of my jobs in Seattle had me working 7:00-3:30 every day, and that was miserable, especially when I relocated and had to be up at 4:00 am to get to work on time. It was *awful*, and I never fully adapted to it.

In Virginia, I was originally 8:00-5:00, but someone in our call center always had to be there from 9:00-6:00 for West Coast customers. Traditionally, my coworkers took turns, but I asked if I could take that shift all the time. They were thrilled and so was I; the extra hour of sleep every day made an enormous difference for me. I still had that constantly jetlagged feeling, but it was better. Definitely more bearable, especially since my sleeping schedule didn't fluctuate anymore.

In fact, one of the reasons I eventually went looking for

another job a few years later was when my boss decided another coworker—one who had childcare issues—would work the 9:00-6:00 shift while I went back to 8:00-5:00. Worse, in order to make it "fair," we alternated weeks. One week I had to be there at 9:00, the next I was there at 8:00. It really threw me off because I just cannot function like that. Unfortunately, people dismiss night owls who struggle to get up early as lazy, and parents take priority over employees without kids, so there was nothing I could do except leave.

Point being, a handful of years with my sleep schedule being uncomfortably off definitely made me very, very guarded about what little sleep I ever get. It also made me wonder if I really wanted to volunteer for the abject misery parents kept describing.

"You'll go *years* without a good night's sleep."

"You will never understand what it means to be tired until you have children."

"No childless/childfree person understands what it means to be sleep-deprived."

Maybe they were just being overly dramatic martyrs. I don't know. What I do know is that it stuck with me—not because I felt sorry for them, but because I wasn't so sure I wanted to volunteer to experience more exhaustion than I already live with.

Could I handle it? Probably. I handled that whole year of getting up at 4:00 am and driving two hours each way to a job that paid me crap and treated me worse, but I wouldn't say I particularly enjoyed it. It was miserable.

Other people handled it, though. And it would be a kid,

not an awful job. So it would be better. It would be worth it. Right?

"It's true, you'll never know love like this," someone said. "But that's a double-edged sword, because this kind of love is incredibly anxious. You're *always* worried. Always. And it never stops. Not even when they're an adult."

Well, that didn't sound appealing at all. I'm a worrier. I'm really good at coming up with worst-case scenarios for *everything*. I've never been officially diagnosed with anxiety, but I would be very surprised if I'm not very firmly on that spectrum.

If I knew I was going to get chewed out at work the next day for some reason, I would be literally sick with worry. Sleep? Not happening. If I'm flying somewhere, I'm at the airport two hours *before* the recommended "arrive two hours early" time because I'm too worried about getting stuck in traffic or otherwise not being there on time. When I go to hockey games, I'm there fully an hour before the gate opens because otherwise I'm too anxious about traffic and finding a place to park. Just that level of anxiety is so uncomfortable and miserable that I'll happily wait around in an airport or stand at the gate of a hockey game for longer than necessary to avoid it.

Now imagine adding parental anxiety to that mess.

I started to ask more questions. I asked a lot of family members, particularly those with young children, what it was like. Considering my absolute lack of experience with small children, I was after any insight I could find. Note that I'm not going to give any details about the people I was speaking with in the name of protecting their privacy.

When I asked what is it about kids that is so much work (an honest question because... lack of experience), a mom said, "You know when you babysat as a teenager? And at the end of the night, you couldn't wait for their parents to come back and take over? It's like that, except no one is coming to take over. It never ends. Ever."

I don't recall exactly what I'd asked another mom—I think it was something about second-guessing my desire to have kids—but I'll never forget her response:

"If you are not absolutely over-the-moon in love with the idea of being a mom... don't."

That one definitely stuck with me... especially because I was starting to realize I *wasn't* over-the-moon in love with the idea anymore.

I was starting to think that maybe I never was.

PART 3

WINDS OF CHANGE

A NEW LIFE, A NEW FUTURE.

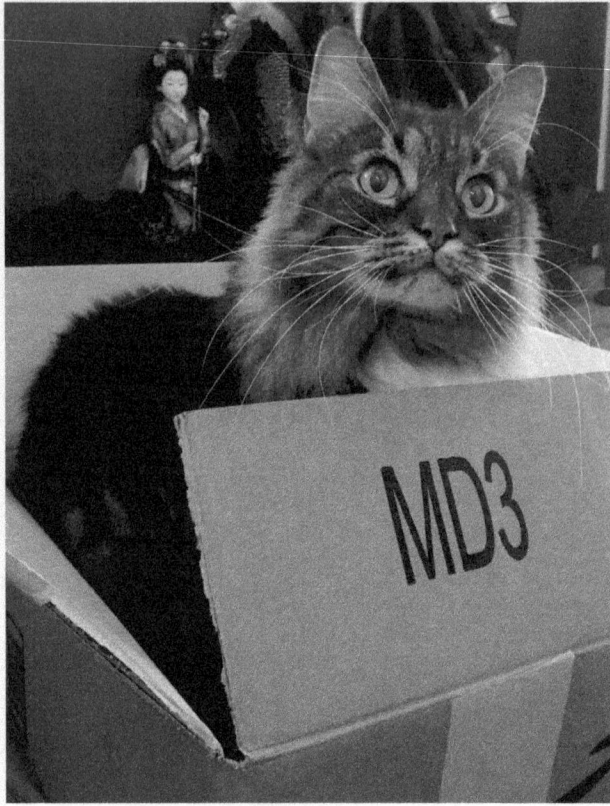

Fluffy in a box. Because cat.

CHAPTER 7

THE TURNING POINT
TWO WEEKS THAT CHANGED EVERYTHING

October of 2006 will always be a strange dot on the timeline of my life. Whenever that month rolls around, the memories flutter in the background, and there's a weird mix of emotions surrounding them. Sometimes it's depressing to think about. Sometimes it's bittersweet—awful memories twined with the understanding that it was also a turning point that altered the course of my life in ways that are undeniably positive.

I can't say I'm glad it happened. I can't say I wish it happened differently. Neither of those statements feels quite right, but they're also both true, for all they're mutually exclusive. Such is the reality of emotions. Nothing is black and white. I wouldn't wish what we went through on our worst enemy, and I would never want to relive it. At the same time, had it not happened, my life would be very different today in ways that I firmly believe I would have found miserable and unfulfilling.

I should mention here that I'm not a believer that things

happen for a reason. I've found far more peace in this world accepting that there is no cosmic rhyme or reason; that much of what happens in life is part of the chaos of an emotionless universe. There is no one manning the controls and deciding what happens to which people. It's not unfair or unjust—it just is.

The chaos of a storm can randomly and unintentionally change the course of a river, and where that river subsequently runs will change—for better or worse—with the arrival of the water. For me, October of 2006 was one of those storms. It redirected the stream in a way I couldn't have envisioned at that time—in a way that was awful and unwanted in the moment—but led to better things later on down the line.

The storm began in early October with something that had become familiar to the point of annoying—a late period. I didn't think much of it because what else was new? I didn't even have to buy a test because I'd bought a three-pack last time to save money. You know the infertility struggle is real when you start buying pregnancy tests in bulk to cut down on costs.

Anyway, we had some plans that weekend where alcohol might be involved. I wasn't much of a drinker, and I'd be driving, so at *most*, I'd be having a drink or two. More than likely, I wouldn't be drinking at all. But hey, why take chances?

So I trooped upstairs to go through the motions. Then I held the plastic stick and, as I had dozens of times before, I watched the little window, waiting for the horizontal line to appear.

But this time, there it was: the vertical line.

A plus, not a minus.

A positive test.

I had always imagined that when this moment came, I'd sprint out of the bathroom and tell Eddie the good news. Picturing that had been one of those things that drove me on. The desire for it to be real pushed me through the discouragement and frustration.

When it came, though, I was still.

Instead of the expected elation, there was disbelief at first. Was I imagining that line? And after trying for so long with no results, I'd honestly started to wonder—even after having one miscarriage—if it was possible for me to get pregnant at all. A positive test didn't seem real.

But no, that line was very, very there. I didn't even have to squint.

Yep. It was real.

Then came the jolt of panic.

I vividly remember the first thought to crystallize:

Oh, shit. There's no turning back now.

I shook that off pretty quickly, though, and then I hurried down to tell Eddie. We were excited and relieved... but that initial moment of panic needled at me. Partly because, I mean, what the hell? I'd wanted this for a long, long time. How could I be upset about it?

But it also needled at me because, well, I wasn't wrong—there *was* no turning back. I thought about that a lot, and I finally chalked it up to a perfectly reasonable amount of fear surrounding pregnancy and childbirth. They are daunting and risky, and I'd done enough reading about all the ways they could go right or wrong to be fully aware that the next several months would be a ride. Once the baby was in, it had to come out sooner or later, one way or another, and I didn't think it was entirely irrational to be nervous about that.

Even after I'd come to terms with that, though, there was still this... discomfort. That was the best way I can describe it. Something wasn't right about my emotions. About my initial reaction, but also in general. This had been the goal for two and a half long years. Why did I have any reservations about it beyond the obvious "this is gonna hurt"?

I didn't dare breathe a word about it to anyone, though. How could I articulate it? How could I explain that even with the excitement and relief, there was this undercurrent of dread and panic—a simultaneous need to slam on the brakes and awareness that it was too late for that? This was what I wanted. What was *wrong* with me?

It also didn't take us long to do the math and realize... Eddie was going to be gone when the baby came. It was currently October, and his ship was due to deploy for six months starting in January. He was understandably disappointed and so was I, but such was the reality of having kids in the military.

The discomfort in the back of my brain swelled a bit more. My mom and I talked about her coming to stay with me toward the end, but that still left quite a bit of time where I'd be on my own. Though we had friends in Norfolk, we didn't have family. I couldn't exactly go back to Seattle because I had a job, a house, pets, etc. I had support, but in a lot of ways, I would be on my own.

Oh, shit, I heard echoing somewhere in my mind. *There's no turning back now.*

A week after the positive test, I was sitting at my desk at work when something suddenly felt... off. I'll spare the details, but there was blood, and I was ultimately put on bedrest to see if things settled down. I knew a few moms who'd been through similar—some bleeding early in pregnancy—and it didn't always mean things were doomed, especially if there was no cramping or clots, which there weren't.

It didn't help that Eddie was at sea during this time. It was a short sea trial—a week or so, if I recall—but those first couple of days, it was just the cats and me.

That got me thinking more and more about his upcoming deployment.

What if there are complications later on? I remember thinking as I lay there. *What if something happens while he's on cruise?*

And even if this was just a bump in the road and everything went smoothly after this, that still meant I was having a baby while my husband was gone. Even if my mom came out to stay with me for a while, sooner or later, Eddie would deploy again. I was signing up to be a single mom for six months at a time. Longer if he ended up going to Iraq or Afghanistan, since those were year-long tours.

There wasn't much I could do about it, though. He was gone right then, and he'd be gone when the baby came, and—as I'd realized when the test showed positive—there was no turning back. One way or the other, we'd just have to make this work.

Eddie came home while I was still on bedrest. By this point, it had been four days of bleeding. Still no sign that a miscarriage was imminent, but also no sign of letting up.

After four days, worry got the best of me, and I decided I should go to the emergency room. At the very least, they could do an ultrasound and see what was going on.

That experience was, unfortunately, yet another addition to my collection of medical trauma. I was freezing cold because the ER was cold, I was wearing a hospital gown, and I'd been bleeding for four days. A corpsman (this was a military hospital) grudgingly brought me a small blanket that didn't do much.

Then one of them announced that the radiologist had been called in to do my ultrasound (it was a Saturday), and I'd need to have a Foley catheter in order to have a full bladder for the procedure. I pushed back, saying they knew an ultrasound would be necessary for at least the past two hours, and they could've given me water during that time. I wasn't risking a UTI with a Foley catheter just because they hadn't bothered to plan, especially since my UTIs were prone to turning into kidney infections.

The corpsman sneered at me and said they wouldn't turn into kidney infections if I treated them appropriately. I responded that the last one had been treated... here.

Finally, I just outright stated that I didn't consent to the Foley catheter, and if they wanted to proceed with the ultrasound, they could bring me some water.

So there I am, wrapped in a thin blanket and a hospital gown, shivering from blood loss in a cold emergency room, and the corpsman brings me... a cup of ice water. As in, a cup with ice all the way to the brim.

From the smirk she gave me, she knew exactly what she was doing.

I looked her right in the eye and drank it anyway. Then, as soon as she left the room, I had Eddie dump the ice in the sink and replace it with tepid water.

When the radiologist arrived, the corpsman triumphantly put the Foley catheter on the gurney so it would be ready to put in once we got to Radiology. The radiologist, she told me, would definitely say it was necessary.

The radiologist was clearly displeased about being called in on her day off, and she made sure the corpsmen knew it. She was polite to me, but I was definitely uncomfortable with her since I knew she was pissed off. So, the ultrasound was not the most pleasant procedure. On the bright side, the corpsman ended up super mad because the radiologist told her the Foley was, in fact, unnecessary. I probably would've laughed at her stomping out of the room if I hadn't been so damn miserable.

In the end, the doctor confirmed the worst—I was miscarrying. Eddie and I were both devastated, of course. Hearing that news crushed me, but it was compounded by the fact that I was already raw and upset from several hours of poor treatment by the corpsmen. I was going through one of the worst and hardest times of my life, and even during the darkest point of that, I still couldn't escape medical trauma. By the time grief entered the picture, I had already been through a completely unnecessary wringer.

Ironically, this happened in the very same facility where the kind ER doctor had restored some of my faith in humanity after Dr. Satan's awful pelvic exam. Military medical giveth and military medical taketh away.

We went home, and I miscarried the next day, which was

Sunday. I was fortunate in that I didn't need a D&C or anything, and it was early enough—about 8 or 9 weeks—that while it was worse than the first miscarriage, it was more emotionally difficult than physically.

That wasn't to say it wasn't physically difficult at all. I'm anemic under the best of circumstances, so the blood loss was taxing. The hormone crash was also unpleasant. Even a few days later, I still felt like I'd been hit by a bus.

But then came Thursday, which was a perfect storm of bullshit I absolutely did not need.

I had to go back to work since I was out of PTO and couldn't afford unpaid leave.

Eddie's ship left that morning for six weeks.

Oh, and it was my birthday. Because of course it was.

My coworkers were great, especially Naomi, a coworker who'd become a close friend. She told me as soon as I arrived that day that if I needed a minute to step outside or something, just let her know and she'd cover for me.

Sometimes I still wonder how I made it through that day. I was nowhere near ready to be there. I was nowhere near ready to be alone for a month and a half.

And I remember going home that night, cuddling with my cats on the couch, and thinking about the big picture.

Did I want to face the prospect of pregnancy and childbirth when I couldn't even miscarry without some medical abuse?

What if I miscarried again, and this time, my husband was gone for the whole thing?

What if everything went perfectly fine, but I was on my own for weeks or months with a new baby?

Obviously, others before me had handled it just fine. My brother was born while my dad was on deployment. We knew plenty of people who'd missed at least one of their kids' births thanks to the military. It was what it was.

But was it what I *wanted?*

More than that, though I wouldn't have admitted it out loud under torture back then, there was a part of me that was relieved. I hated myself for it. I felt guilty and ashamed. I didn't want to feel like I'd dodged a bullet or that I had a second chance to consider how I wanted to move forward... but I did.

More and more, I thought about that recurring feeling of *Oh, shit, there's no turning back now.* Sometimes I felt awful —as if I'd manifested the miscarriage by having intrusive thoughts—but other times, I wondered if it was a gut feeling I should listen to. If the miscarriage and the upcoming deployment were an opportunity to reevaluate the future.

And little by little, the undercurrent of doubt—the one that had been there steadily since the positive test—started to get louder.

CHAPTER 8

ANCHORS AWEIGH

SIX MONTHS TO THINK THINGS THROUGH.

Ask anyone who's spent any time around the Navy, and they'll tell you that a six-month deployment isn't *just* six months. The actual cruise is six months, but before the ship leaves for that cruise, there are sea trials and workups. The ship goes out for a few days or a few weeks at a time, usually in progressively longer increments leading up to the deployment.

This workup cycle was well underway when I miscarried, and Eddie left for six weeks just days afterward.

During that time, I was obviously still recovering from everything. Mostly mentally and emotionally; physically, I was more or less back to normal after a week or two. Exhausted and a little anemic for obvious reasons, but there wasn't a whole lot of pain. And the hormone crash was... fun. I'd have recovered even faster if I hadn't had to return to work too soon, but hey, capitalism. My psychological recovery also lagged in part because of this; nothing helps someone bounce back like getting chewed out by customers.

But I digress.

By around mid-November, I was still depressed about it all, not to mention missing my husband. Mostly, I was able to function like an adult, and I even joined an online writing community just to give myself something else to focus on. I was about to have six months on my hands—might as well get back to writing, right? That was probably one of the best things I did for myself during that period. It gave me something to look forward to even while I dreaded my husband being away for half a year.

But then one morning, I woke up and could barely get out of bed. Physically, I felt all right in the sense that nothing hurt. I just... couldn't will myself to move.

Somehow, I managed to drag myself up. Now that I was upright, I thought I'd shake it off. I was a lifelong insomniac, so I figured this was just the hangover from a bad night of sleep.

I didn't shake it off. I had to force myself to do every little thing—showering, eating, driving, working. It was exhausting, which only made the just-got-hit-by-a-truck feeling worse. The closest thing I could liken it to was some of the worst bouts of depression I'd gone through over the years. I've experienced executive dysfunction before and since, and this was like the worst executive dysfunction on steroids. There were moments when it genuinely felt like even if I could convince myself to go through the motions of something simple— making a sandwich, driving to work—I wasn't 100% sure my brain would actually make my body do it. It's difficult to describe, but it's *awful*.

Naturally, I got concerned, and I also had an uncomfortable inkling that I knew what this was. I started making calls to Beth and John, and long story short, that was how I learned it *is* possible to get postpartum depression after a miscarriage.

Of course, people barely believe PPD exists, so I wasn't at all surprised when mine was dismissed. People told me, "Nah, it's just grief," and "Well, of course you're sad after a miscarriage." This was different, though.

It also made me understand why new mothers feel so alone and frustrated when they have PPD. At least I was *expected* to be sad and depressed. A new mom gets a pass for being tired, but depressed? Unhappy? Sad? You just had a *baby*, madam! You should be *glowing* with happiness!

If I learned anything from this experience, it was just how serious, how real, and how *chemical* PPD really is. I was grieving, but I wasn't sleep-deprived, recovering from childbirth, nursing, and responsible for an infant that was constantly demanding something from me. PPD on top of all of that sounds absolutely brutal to me, and I sincerely hope that if you take only one thing away from this book, it's how real PPD is. If a new mom in your orbit is showing signs of it, please reach out and make sure they're getting the help they need. It's no joke.

The experience also got me thinking—what if this means I'm prone to PPD? What if I had to take care of a baby right now when I was genuinely struggling to take care of myself? What if when I do have a baby, I get hit even harder with this?

And slowly, another crack began to form in the foundation of my desire to be a mother.

———————

One blessing in disguise of the workups/deployment happening right after the miscarriage was that it gave me time for some serious soul-searching.

I also decided that since I had six months to myself, I might as well make the best of them rather than moping around and counting down the days until Eddie came home. I hadn't really had that opportunity last time he was deployed; I would leave at 4:15 am, get home at 6:00 pm, and have to be in bed by 8:30 in order to get up the next morning. I spent most of that deployment just trying to stay awake.

This time, when I'd expected to be getting ready for a baby, I had six months to fill with whatever I wanted. Working, obviously, but outside of that forty hours a week, I had options. It also occurred to me that this was probably the last time I'd have this opportunity, since there was a good chance I'd be pregnant or have a baby by the *next* deployment.

So... why not be a little selfish and focus on me?

As I mentioned before, I joined an online writing forum. I was determined to start taking the craft more seriously and move more definitively in the direction of becoming an author. Not necessarily full-time, but getting published was the dream. Now I had the time. Might as well use it.

I also started going to the gym regularly. Naomi went almost daily and knew a lot about cardio and weight training, and she took me under her wing. I started going with her once a week and on my own three or four days. It got me out of the house and got me doing something physical, and it felt good. Okay, it didn't *always* feel good; Naomi did *not* go easy on me. But I digress.

"In the future," I told myself more than once, "I'm going to have to have a babysitter when I do this. Especially if Eddie is at sea."

Yeah, that was probably true. But I didn't have to have one right then, so I enjoyed the freedom to go to the gym four to five times a week without worrying about logistics beyond clean workout clothes and a water bottle.

At least once or twice a week, I'd go to a particular Vietnamese restaurant not far from the gym after my workout. One of my favorite parts of the evening was chilling with a bowl of Phở and a book.

I don't think a single one of these dinners passed without me thinking, *"I wouldn't be able to do this with a baby."*

Sure, people took their kids out to dinner, but it wasn't a quiet, leisurely dinner spent reading.

That was not, I was beginning to realize despite my best efforts, how I wanted to spend my dinners.

―――――――――

Eddie's deployment wasn't *all* about freedom and sleeping in.

Near the end, I got hellaciously sick one week. I was so sick I couldn't eat and I could barely function. Naturally, it happened on my much-anticipated weeklong staycation (what a waste of five PTO days), so at least I didn't have to call in sick to work. Silver linings and all that.

Lying in bed on day three or four, trying to will myself to go downstairs and put some food into my face, it occurred to me that if things had happened differently, I'd have been almost eight months pregnant at that point. And what if I got sick like this while I had a baby or a toddler, especially while my husband was gone?

Yes, other people manage it, but was it something I really wanted to do?

As it was, I was happy that my cats were fairly self-sufficient. I checked their food and water daily, and I tried to stay on top of the litter box as much as I could that week, but they're pretty low-maintenance creatures. They didn't need to go outside. They didn't need walks. They were free fed, so they didn't need to be fed at specific times. Even a dog would've been too much for me that week.

Could I have taken care of a baby during that time? Probably.

Did I want to have that responsibility when I was struggling to take care of myself? Not really, no.

There were a lot of little realizations like that during the six months that Eddie was gone. It was like my desire to be a mom was being subjected to death by a thousand cuts. From being sick to going to restaurants, it wasn't so much realizing that everyday things were insurmountable or impossible with kids. It was just the steady epiphany that while I might have been capable of dealing with those things as a parent, I simply... didn't want to.

The life I'd be choosing if I became a mother...

Do you want that, Lori? Do you really?

I was having a harder and harder time stubbornly

dismissing those questions and saying, "Of course I do. Having a kid will be worth the hard stuff."

As I mentioned earlier, I'd decided to spend the deployment writing more earnestly, and I'd done so. I was frustrated with my job for myriad reasons, and I felt like I was doing nothing with my life. Writing was a way of finding meaning and purpose, and it was a way of coping with the grief—since I wasn't going to have a baby during this time, then I was damn sure going to use the time to do *something* worthwhile. I always gravitated toward writing, so that was what I did now.

I'd haul my laptop to restaurants, and in between eating, I'd pluck away at my book. (I also tipped generously to make up for staying a little longer than if I'd just eaten dinner) I spent hours on end writing on the weekends, and even at work, I kept a notebook where I could jot little ideas to get them out of my head. I was immersing myself in my writing more than I had in years, and I was loving it.

In fact, the only thing I didn't like about the deployment was that Eddie was gone. I missed him. But the way I was living while he was on deployment—this was how I *liked* to live.

I much preferred it when he was there with me, but things didn't really change then. We'd go to the gym together. We'd take impromptu trips if budgets and work schedules allowed. We'd have long, indulgent dinners in restaurants and sleep in on Saturdays.

I *liked* my life by myself, and I *liked* our life together.

The fact was, I had to consider my life by myself as much as I considered my life with Eddie. That's the reality of being a military spouse—you're going to be alone for long stretches. At the time, there was also a very real possibility of him being sent into Iraq or Afghanistan for boots-on-the-ground combat. It was still voluntary for the Navy, but that could change. If it did, then I'd be looking at twelve-month stretches on my own instead of six-month, and also the possibilities of him being traumatized, injured, or worse.

By being a milspouse, those were part of my reality. And much like everything in my world right then, that too was interrogated with regard to parenthood.

Did I want to be a single mother for six to twelve months at a stretch?

Was I equipped to handle whatever the war did to my husband while also taking care of kids?

That made me think more about the big picture of being a military family. While I was fortunate in that I was a stationary Navy brat—my dad never moved after I was born—my parents both moved around a lot as kids. My mom was a Navy brat, too. I have cousins who spent their formative years bouncing all over the U.S. as well as overseas. I met many military families in Norfolk who'd PCSed[1] multiple times. And you know what? It's hard! It's tough on kids, especially, and it's tough on parents who have to deal with all the headache associated with PCSing, *plus* doing it with kids.

Had things played out differently back in October, I'd soon be adopting the life of being a single parent during deployments and while navigating a PCS with kids. It was the life of the parents at the next table who were trying to keep one kid quiet and encourage the other to just *try* the spring rolls. The life of someone who needed a babysitter to go to the gym and who didn't have long periods of uninterrupted writing time.

And more and more... I wasn't so sure I *wanted* that life.

I *liked* being able to leave the house on a moment's notice without much preparation. Wallet, keys, phone—off I'd go! No diaper bag. No car seat. No making sure there were toys, snacks, diapers, extra clothes, or anything else.

I *liked* going to the gym on my own time, taking as little or as long as I wanted, and then having whatever I wanted for dinner afterward.

I *liked* taking off after work on Friday to drive to another state, hang out with a friend, go to a model horse show, and then come back on Sunday to cats who were fine on their own.

I *liked* going to bed as early or late as I wanted to, sleeping in on a weekend if I felt like it, and indulging in an all-day Law & Order: SVU marathon once in a while.

I *liked* taking my laptop to a restaurant and writing while I ate.

And I *liked* being able to wallow completely and be fully pathetic while I was sick, resting and taking it easy until I was back on my feet.

But I couldn't quite make myself commit to saying I didn't want kids. We'd spent so much time and so much money trying, and it felt like a failure to say, "You know what? Never mind." (Ahh, good ol' sunk-cost fallacy)

I also knew that there was no compromising when it came to having kids. It's just not possible. So if I decided I didn't want them, but Eddie still did...

Well, let's just say that by the time he came back from deployment, I was at a mental crossroads.

And though the childfree life called to me like a siren, fear is a strong motivator. I was afraid of regrets, and of giving up after all that time, money, and energy. I just couldn't admit to myself that maybe this wasn't what I wanted.

Despite my increasing reservations, I remained determined to become a mother.

Sort of.

CHAPTER 9

EYES WIDE OPEN
THE EPIPHANY

In the months after Eddie's deployment, I did some more heavy soul-searching. A huge part of that involved taking an unfiltered look at my past—at who I'd been over time—and what that said about my desire to be a parent.

As kids do, I had a lot of fleeting ideas about my future. We all know kids who want to be a firefighter one week, an astronaut the next, etc., and I was no different. I had all kinds of career dreams, some of which lasted for years while others fizzled after a relatively brief period.

One of those dreams was constant, though. In fact, my parents once commented that from the time I was very young, my career plans were always, "I want to be X... or a writer."

"I want to be a marine biologist... or a writer."

"I want to be a film director... or a writer."

"I want to be a psychologist... or a writer."

The truth was, being a writer was *always* the dream. No matter what I did for a living, I would be a writer. Sometimes

I entertained the idea of writing as a career, but that was usually shot down by the pragmatic adults in my life (teachers, mostly) who assured me that it was virtually impossible to make a living as a writer. They'd tell me to be a journalist if I really wanted to make money writing, but I knew from a very, very young age that journalism wasn't for me. I wanted to write fiction. I wanted to write *novels*. Come hell or high water, I was going to do exactly that.

During the last couple of years I lived in Norfolk, I would spend my commute to and from work (about thirty minutes each way) thinking about how much I wanted to be doing something else. Even before I decided I was unhappy with my job—when I was more or less okay with where I worked and what I was doing—I would still think, "Is this it? Is this all I'm going to do with my life?"

And when I'd imagine a life *after* this job—when I'd imagine doing something *more*—I wouldn't think about being a mom. I would dream about writing. That included during the most frustrating periods when I wanted this whole infertility thing to be over—I didn't envision babies and kids. I envisioned writing.

But that was most likely a fantasy. I understood very early on that making a living as a writer was a crapshoot, so I always had a primary career goal in mind. From the time I was very young, even though I didn't voice this to people for fear of being laughed at, I viewed every potential career through a lens of "Will I still be able to write?" If a job was so physically and/or mentally taxing that I'd have nothing left for writing, then it wasn't a good career for me. If it required so many hours that I simply wouldn't have time to write, then it was also out.

All my life, everything I envisioned for my future carved out space and time to write.

You know what *didn't* get consideration when I thought about my future?

Kids.

I kind of assumed the whole marriage-and-kids thing would happen just because that seemed to be what everyone did. I was well into my teens before I realized kids were completely optional, and I quickly jumped on the idea of being childfree. Nothing about it appealed to me. *Nothing*.

When I read about writers who made it work around kids and demanding careers, I thought, *okay,* they *made it work, but I know me, and I won't be able to do that.*

After all, I was acutely aware of my limits, which is one of the reasons I want to tell the following story.

When I was in high school, my state offered the Running Start program. This allowed high school students to take classes at a community college during their junior and senior years. As my guidance counselor explained it, for every five credits (one class) I took at the college, I'd need to drop two classes at the high school. So if I took a full-time load (fifteen credits), then I'd need to stop coming to high school completely.

His intent was to talk me out of doing Running Start by showing me that I'd miss out on the social aspects of high school. This backfired on him—I realized everything he was telling me was just recommendations, and he could not, in fact, stop me from taking a full-time load at *both* schools.

So for my junior year, I was taking fifteen to twenty credits at the college while also taking four or five classes at my high school. I eased off the gas a little during my senior year, but I still took enough that I graduated high school with an Associate's Degree in hand.

Doing a double full-time load meant school ran from 7:30 am until 10:00 pm, plus I had to drive twenty-five miles each way to the college, so I'd commute between schools 2:00-3:00 pm and get home around 11:00. During this time, I still maintained friendships, even had some boyfriends, and managed to stay relatively sane.

So when I say I know my limits, I'm not joking. I also know that I can only sustain that for a finite period of time; by the end of each quarter, I was usually ready to collapse, and when I graduated, I was burned out enough that I put off finishing my bachelor's. I can go hard and run myself into the ground, but I can't do it in the long term. Even back then, when people talked about the first few years of a kid's life—the sleep deprivation and constant exhaustion, usually while also holding down a job—a little voice in my head said, "I'm not wired for that." I had firsthand knowledge of how much I could truly handle, and it was about eleven to twelve weeks of full speed ahead before I had to take a break. And that was with weekends and the ability to sleep through the night! (Well, as much as I ever sleep through the night)

Looking back at that, comparing my experience with sleep deprivation, stress, and burnout with everything being a parent promised... I asked myself that question yet again:

Was motherhood what I wanted?

No. No, it really wasn't.

The other reason I'm telling this story is that attending college for those two years meant being exposed to people from all walks of life. Particularly since I was taking night classes, the vast majority of my classmates were significantly older than me. There were service members from the nearby Navy base, workers from Boeing, teachers doing continuing education, blue collar workers, white collar workers, nursing students, etc., and lots and *lots* of parents. Single parents, married parents, stepparents, teen parents, grandparents— you name it.

At seventeen, I was going to class with people who had to scramble to find childcare. One of my classmates had to bring her baby to class and take an exam out in the hall because the baby kept fussing. People occasionally brought young kids with them, set them up with coloring books in the back row, and tried to concentrate on the lecture while keeping an eye on their kids. Some had adult kids. It was truly a mix.

I've often said that the most profound education from that period in my life didn't come from the textbooks and lectures so much as it did from my classmates. These were people who were neck deep in real life. I'd usually end up with a small group of friends to hang out with in the commons before our classes started, and those conversations offered peeks into lives vastly different from my or my high school classmates' lives.

Some of the biggest things that stuck with me were the comments they'd make about their own lives as parents, or how they'd remark about my future plans through the lens of their lived experience. When I'd mention that I wanted to travel, or that I wanted to write a book, or that I wanted to get a graduate degree, it was not uncommon at all for someone to very seriously tell me, "Do that *before* you have kids." Or they'd talk about the dreams they'd had when they were young, and with a sigh, they'd add, "But now I have kids."

These people clearly loved their kids, but I often got the impression they didn't love their *lives*.

I wanted to love my life.

So fast forward to 2008, and I'm rethinking the life I have, the life I want, and the life I've been trying to kick start for over the past few years.

And I realize... I don't think I want this.

It was never something I wanted when I was a kid. It was something I actively eschewed as a teenager. Now, as a married twentysomething, I realized none of those feelings had changed. I still didn't want it.

In fact, somewhere along the line in our infertility struggle, I'd stopped wanting a baby at all. The desire for one had been fleeting in retrospect; maybe I'd just been caught up in the excitement of getting married? I still don't really know. It was never "well, this is the next step" because I had long since broken away from the idea that it *was* the next step. For whatever reason, I'd wanted a baby.

The Infertility Fairy had shown up and stuck around, and now that I was rethinking everything, I realized I didn't want a baby—I just wanted the infertility to be over. The arrival of a baby was a means to an end, not the beginning of a life I was looking forward to living.

A baby deserved better than that, and so did I.

But was I making the right decision? Because now I was second-guessing everything, especially since there was a very real possibility this could be the end of my marriage. You can't compromise on kids. If one partner wants them and one doesn't, there's no middle ground.

First things first, I needed a sounding board just to make sure I was making sense.

At work that day, I pulled aside a coworker, and I finally said the words out loud: "I don't think I actually want kids."

I was fully prepared for all the usual retorts that childfree people get, and probably a reminder that her kids were the light of her life, and that we'd worked so hard to get this far, etc.

I was not at all ready when her face lit up and she said, "Oh, thank God. I love my kids more than life itself, but if I could go back..."

What followed was her admitting that she was 100% supportive of us and our struggle, and she would've celebrated with us if we'd had a baby. She'd never in a million years try to talk someone out of having one. but now that I was having doubts, she urged me to grab on to that and hold on. I hadn't crossed a point of no return, and she encouraged me to do what she wished she'd done—say no while I still could.

With that outside validation came the realization that my doubts weren't just cold feet. There was a small voice in my head getting louder by the minute, and I needed to listen to it. By the time we'd finished talking, the question had become a statement:

"I don't want kids?"

"I don't want kids."

Now... the fun part.

I sat down with Eddie, and I told him the same thing I'd told my coworker, only with more conviction this time: "I really don't want kids anymore."

He was surprised, and he said, "Well, can we talk about this?"

I said we could, but I was still sure this would be the end of us. As I said, there's no compromising here. If he still wanted kids, I'd let him go with no hard feelings, but I wasn't looking forward to it.

We decided to go out to dinner to talk things over, and we picked a favorite restaurant out in Virginia Beach. It was the Vietnamese restaurant I frequented after going to the gym; a place we both knew very well. This was where I think the universe may have had a sense of humor: this usually quiet restaurant was *absolutely crawling with children*. Mostly toddlers and slightly older. So. Many. Children.

Eddie looked around the restaurant. Then he looked at me and said, "I wonder how difficult it is to get a vasectomy."

We both laughed, which broke some tension, and then we started discussing the reality of the situation. I explained the reasons why I didn't think kids were for me. The more we talked, the more Eddie seemed to warm up to the idea, too.

Neither of us was ready to take any permanent steps. He wanted some time to think, and even though I was more sure of this than I had been about anything in a long time, I wanted to give it some more thought, too.

The conversation ran deeper than just whether we wanted kids. In fact, we realized that while we were very happy together, we were incredibly unhappy with the life we had. For a long time, we'd both thought it was just the underlying stress of infertility, but no. It was everything. We hated our jobs. We hated living in Norfolk. The life we had there wasn't what we wanted. Not in the short-term, and definitely not in the long-term.

We weren't quite sure how, but we knew without a doubt that we needed to change a lot of things. We needed to change almost everything.

One year later, our world would be completely different.

CHAPTER 10

MORE CHANGING TIDES

After that conversation in early 2008, we knew we needed to change a lot of things about our life. The question was... how?

Changing my job would be reasonably easy. Find a new job, give my two weeks' notice, start the new job. But it was hard to say if I'd find much improvement. What I needed was a *career*. I started looking into certification programs. Massage therapy was calling to me, and I began reading up on training and local schools.

Changing *Eddie's* job wasn't going to be so simple.

Or, well, that was what we thought.

Some dumb luck and good timing landed him a temporary assignment to his ship's security department. He found he enjoyed that more than what he was already doing (aviation electronics), and with his reenlistment coming up, he thought he might cross-rate permanently. For the non-military folks, your rate is your job. At the moment, he was an AT (aviation electronics tech), and he was very interested in switching to MA (master-at-arms; basically a cop).

As it happened, the Navy was also very interested in people cross-rating to MA at that time. In fact, they were offering a substantial reenlistment bonus for people who did so. Given that he already wanted to cross-rate and we were *broke*, the offer was too enticing to pass up.

Just a handful of months after that fateful conversation, it was done: he had orders to MA school, and when he completed school, he'd reenlist with that tasty bonus.

Around that same time, I had finally gotten fed up with my job, and while I was still considering more permanent career options, it was time to move on to something else. After sending out some applications and doing some interviews on my lunch breaks, I landed a job as a manager at a car rental company. It was a significant raise, plus the job included a free car and free gas. Considering this was summer of 2008 when gas spiked to $4/gallon, free gas was an *amazing* perk. The job was tough and demanding, but I liked it, and it paid well.

I had *just* finished training and was on my second day actually working in the lot when I got a call from Eddie. Apparently he had just gotten off the phone with the detailer.

In the military, when you're reenlisting or changing duty stations, your orders are issued by a detailer. Usually, you can give them a few options of places you'd like to go, and sometimes they'll actually send you to one of them.

I don't remember exactly why, but the detailer told him, "You have a choice—Guam, Bahrain, or Okinawa—and you have to make the decision *now*."

Fortunately, since we'd caught wind that MAs were often sent overseas, Eddie and I had spent some time looking at the various overseas bases and deciding where, given the choice, we'd like to go. Among our top choices? Okinawa.

So here I am, day two of actually working my job, and Eddie said, "We have four months to report to Okinawa."

They weren't kidding, either, and the logistics of moving to Okinawa is *not* for the faint of heart. Advanced level: taking *pets* to Okinawa. Japan is a rabies free zone, and they are *extremely* strict about screening animals. That entire debacle could probably be its own book.

Don't worry, though—two kitties made it safely to Japan with us, and the other two lived happily with my parents. The Navy would only let us take two, and we could only have two in base housing, but it worked out okay because I don't think our boys would've tolerated the trip well. It was hard to leave them behind, but it really was the best solution for everybody.

There was also the super fun task of driving all four kitties across the United States from Norfolk to Seattle. That's a little under three thousand miles. With four cats.

"Thank God," we said to each other multiple times on that trip, "we don't have kids."

Is it doable with kids? Absolutely. People PCS overseas with kids all the time. But we were at our limit with the cats and more than a little grateful we didn't have to handle transferring with kids too. My hat is off to those who do it. It's just not for us.

Now, as we were getting everything squared away to move halfway around the world, we also looked ahead to what waited for us on the island. As it happened, I'd already done a little research about the bases on Okinawa while we'd been considering our overseas options, but now I dug deeper to see what we were really getting into. Service members and dependents gave it mixed reviews. A lot of people said it was boring and there was nothing to do. People complained about the food. Others really liked it.

One thing I did learn very quickly was that jobs were not readily available over there. The U.S. military has an agreement with host countries that results in the 70-30 rule (or 60-40, depending on the country). What this means is that for every three American civilians hired on-base, seven local nationals must be hired (or six locals for every four Americans if it's a 60-40 country). We're also not allowed to work off-base.

So for most dependents, the options are:

- Work in the Exchange or commissary, which are subject to the 70-30 rule.
- Work in one of the on-base restaurants, which are also subject to the rule.
- Offer in-home childcare.
- Run a multi-level marketing "business."

I'm not joking about that last one, either. MLMs are extremely prevalent on military bases for a lot of reasons, and they seem to be even more pervasive overseas where spouses have few options.

The next time I talked to Eddie, I told him about this. I

said, "There are almost no jobs over there. I'm not sure what to do."

He thought for a moment. Then he replied, "When we got married, you said that if we ever had the means, you wanted to try taking 6-12 months off from working to get your writing career going. Looks like you have three years."

I was actually kind of dazed after I got off the phone. This was a once in a lifetime opportunity. For the first time in my adult life, I had a purpose and a direction that I was absolutely sure about. No question. I wasn't sure *how* I was going to make it work or how much money I'd actually be able to make, but one way or another, my professional writing career was *going* to start on Okinawa. For the next couple of months, I'd work on tying up loose ends in Norfolk and dealing with all the logistics of PCSing.

Once I landed on that island, though? It was game on.

I'll get to that in a minute, because transitioning to Japan wasn't *all* smooth sailing. You may recall that I mentioned this was summer of 2008. Folks of a certain age may remember that there was more going on than just gas prices shooting up—the real estate bubble burst.

We, following the advice of everyone who said you *cannot* lose by buying a house and that it was the smartest investment you could *ever* make, had purchased a house in 2005.

I'm sure you can see where this is going.

Fortunately, we had a fixed rate mortgage, so we didn't get snowed under by exploding mortgage payments. Unfortunately, we were heading overseas, which meant we were losing both my income and our housing allowance. *Also* unfortunately, our house lost like half its value overnight, so we couldn't sell the place.

The reenlistment bonus would tide us over for a while. We also managed to get tenants to rent the place, though thanks to the tanking market, we could only charge about half the mortgage for rent.

This would wind up being an epic saga that dragged on from 2008 through 2014, until the bank finally screwed us out of a short sale and we lost the house via a deed-in-lieu of foreclosure.

Good thing real estate is always a great investment.

Anyway, I won't get in that entire debacle except to say that it was part of a perfect storm that had us seriously struggling financially while we lived in Japan. There was one month where we literally had $20 to carry us through an entire two-week pay period. We started what we called our "Zombie stash"—cheap, non-perishable food we bought over time, building up a stash in case money got even tighter (or in case the zombies came, which sounded way cooler). We kept extra cat food and litter around just in case, too.

Push came to shove, we have a great support system—if we were truly desperate, my parents would (and did) help us.

But that was an incredibly lean period in our lives.

And I remember thinking, almost daily...

Thank God we don't have to feed or clothe kids right now.

Money was definitely tight, but we *loved* living on Okinawa. It truly is a beautiful island. The food is spectacular. We visited Ryukyu castles, World War II historical sites, shrines, and every UNESCO World Heritage site on the island. We visited the caves at Okinawa World. We checked out the pineapple farm, Kokusai Street, and every beach we could find. The island is tiny— it's about eighteen miles wide at its widest point and less than seventy miles long. It's literally smaller than Long Island. But there was so much to see and do that when my parents came to visit, we ran them *ragged* trying to show them everything over three weeks.

The snorkeling is so incredible that when we went snorkeling off Maui a few years later, we both thought, "Eh, that's it?" because it just didn't compare to the water off Oki. If you ever have the chance to visit that tiny island, I highly, highly recommend it.

We didn't have a lot of money, but it was just the two of us, and we had the time of our lives.

And there on that island, with no jobs available and no kids, I finally became the person I'd always dreamed I would be.

PART 4

CHILDFREE

I'll be 40 with a bunch of cats?
Don't threaten me with a good time.

CHAPTER 11

AUTHOR AT LAST

WHO I WAS ALWAYS SUPPOSED TO BE

One of the common comments childfree people hear is that it's shallow, selfish, and short-sighted to prioritize a career over a family. A career won't love us, won't take care of us when we're old, won't keep us company on our deathbed, etc.

But for some of us, the careers we find really *are* the purpose we need.

Throughout my life, even through the years of infertility, I can honestly say I never truly connected with the purpose people find in parenthood. While I could appreciate and even want the big picture—the adult kids with fully-formed minds and lives—I never vibed with the trappings of raising kids. I never really knew how to interact with little kids as an adult. As a teenager, babysitting was something I did to make extra money, but given the choice between that and cleaning horse stalls... gimme the pitchfork.

Writing, though? I was all over that. I was drawn to author events, writing classes, books on the craft, and anything and everything I could get my hands on that related to writing. My grandmother would accumulate stacks of Writer's Digest and give them to me, and I'd pore over them until the pages were ragged. I *lived* for creative writing assignments at school. Writing has been my passion ever since I first understood that someone had to write the stories I read when I was little. I wanted to write. I *needed* to write.

From the time I could string a sentence together, I was writing short stories. I hated writing longhand, but my family had a PC with Word5 on it (yeah, I know, I'm aging myself). I knew my way around a word processor before I knew how to play Super Mario Bros (good Lord, I really am old). By the time I was in fourth grade, I was plotting out novels, and my parents and teachers encouraged it. I finished a book—probably novella length—in sixth grade, and I kept writing short stories and novellas all through school.

When I was in high school and college, I spent ages on an epic fantasy novel. All told, I ended up writing it three times —the first time a year or two after I graduated high school, the second during Eddie's 2007 deployment, and again just before we went to Okinawa in 2008. That book will never see the light of day, but the 500,000+ words I wrote between those three drafts taught me about story structure, pacing, character development, dialogue, plotting, etc. I developed an outlining method and a template for tracking my word counts that I still use today.

It was shortly after I finished that third draft (and around the time I realized it was unpublishable dreck) that we got our orders to Okinawa. This would also be the beginning of my writing career, though I could not have envisioned back then the way it would all play out.

As I'd promised myself, I started writing as soon as I landed on Okinawa.

Actually, it started before that. I was due to fly out in mid-November, and in October, I decided to embark on NaNoWriMo. That's National Novel Writing Month, where the goal is to write 50,000 words in a month. Since I am the queen of ADHD and procrastination, I thought this would be a good way for me to discipline myself and get into the habit of writing daily.

Since I had two weeks before NaNo actually kicked off, I didn't think I had time to plot out an epic fantasy, which was what I'd been writing up to this point. So I thought, well, romance is relatively simple, at least compared to epic fantasy. It was far more doable to plot one in two weeks and write it in 30 days.

November 1st came, and I banged out over 10,000 words my first day. By the time I landed on Okinawa, I was almost finished with the book, and I hit the 50,000-word goal before I'd even moved out of temporary housing.

Through this process, I learned that writing romance was a lot of fun! So, I plotted and wrote another. Then another. I was afraid to lose the momentum I'd built during NaNo, so I kept going. Somewhere in my second or third book, I started keeping track of my word counts on a spreadsheet, and I found that 5,000 words per day was a sustainable pace for me.

As they say, if it ain't broke, don't fix it—what I was doing was working, so I kept going.

I'm not joking about that, either—it's now 2024, and my daily quota is still 5,000 words per day. I don't write every single day, mostly because I have administrative tasks and editing to deal with, and because I've also learned to have a better work-life balance, but I usually write between 80-100,000 words per month.

Much like my husband cross-rating within the Navy, there was some good luck and good timing involved in my career. I happened to start submitting to publishers around the time eBooks were becoming popular. I also lucked into the gay romance genre around the time it was picking up steam. I landed some contracts with small publishers, my books hit the market, and they started to sell.

So, how did it pan out as a job?

Better than I expected, that was for sure. After all those years of being told "You can't make a living as a writer" in between "You'll never be as fulfilled by a career as you would by motherhood," I steadily shifted from a few royalties trickling in to a respectable and somewhat consistent income.

The first year we lived on Okinawa, we discovered an amazing restaurant called Sam's by the Sea. Fantastic steak place with a Polynesian theme and the most incredible curry soup on the planet. But for a couple of poor kids living on an E5 salary (read: not much) with a mortgage back in the U.S., going to Sam's was a rare treat. We'd even have to negotiate whether we could order appetizers (Lord, their tempura cheese sticks are *divine*), and if we dared to order one of the mocktails that came with a souvenir cup (about $10-12, if I recall).

In late 2009, just over a year after I arrived on the island, my first two books came out and the first royalty checks came in. We celebrated by going to Sam's. It was the first time we had appetizers *and* souvenir cup mocktails. After a solid year of stretching every dollar, it felt like we were living the high life.

2010 saw a steady shift from "Ooh, we can afford to go to Sam's!" to "Yo, we've already been to Sam's this month, but we can actually swing another trip."

The first time we went to Sam's twice in the *same week* was in 2011, and while that sounds like a silly little thing, it felt big to us. It felt like things were changing, and not in a flash in the pan, blip on the radar kind of way. Like we were leaving behind the "can we afford ground beef and milk to make Hamburger Helper?" and dipping our toes into the world of "we went to the commissary this morning and we can go to Sam's tonight."

At the end of 2011, when I returned to the States, I had doubled the income from my last job. It doubled again in 2012, and has stayed at or above that amount ever since.

So much for "you can't make a living as a writer."

For the first time, I didn't have that panicked feeling that my life was passing me by and leaving me behind. I'd always been frustrated at my jobs because I was spinning my tires and not getting anywhere, and that anywhere I *could* go in those jobs wasn't somewhere I wanted to be. I didn't have that frustrated, flailing feeling of trying to figure out who I was, what I wanted, and what I wanted to do with my life.

No, I wasn't raking in millions of dollars. No, Hollywood wasn't knocking down my door for movie rights. At that point, I wasn't even working with any of the Big Five publishers[1].

But I was writing books, publishing them, and paying my bills with the royalties. People were *reading* my books. I was an *author*.

Not only that, I was a *full-time* author. More than I'd ever let myself believe was possible, I was living the dream I'd had since my age was in the single digits.

This was, and remains today, everything I could ever want and then some.

This was fulfillment.

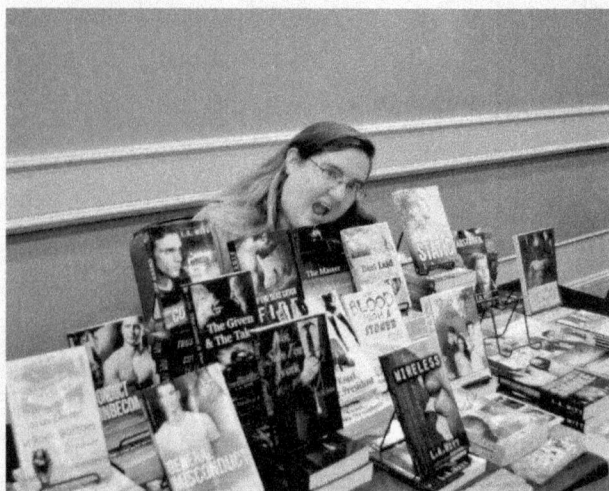

Being a consummate professional at a book event.
(I don't remember who took this photo.)

CHAPTER 12

WHEN NO ONE ELSE IS LISTENING

WHAT PARENTS SAY ABOUT PARENTHOOD

I want to revisit the things parents say, this time through the lens of someone who's firmly childfree, rather than infertile or on the fence. Because what people say and how they say it definitely does change—for better or worse—when a person has chosen not to have kids.

I absolutely advocate asking parents to be candid about the realities of parenthood. If you have someone in your life who you can trust to be honest and open about things, by all means—ask!

Sometimes, however, it's good to just sit back and listen. Really, really listen to what parents are saying—both the things they mean to say, and the subtext they probably don't intend to let slip. Because when they're not on the spot or feeling like they have to keep up the June Cleaver façade, you'd be amazed the insights they'll offer. The second they catch the scent that they're turning you off to parenthood, though, the tune changes immediately.

For example, I had more variations of this conversation than I can count:

Parent: "Once you have kids, you'll *never* get enough sleep. If you're not a parent, you don't even know what tired *means*." (Variant: "If you're not a parent, you're not allowed to ever complain about being tired.")

Me, already a lifelong insomniac: "Oh. Huh. Well, that doesn't sound appealing. I'll pass."

Parents: "What!? How can you skip parenthood? Kids are the best thing ever!"

So, while I was on the fence about actually having kids, I started just... not saying anything. Or at least not tipping my hand that their comments were making me second guess my desire to become a parent.

Instead, I let them talk.

"Parenting is so hard," they'd say. "It's the hardest thing ever. You'll never understand how hard it is until you do it."

I still didn't quite understand what was so hard about being a parent. Not that it wasn't difficult, just that... I couldn't quite connect with why it was *so hard*.

I constantly heard parents talking about how hard it was, but I didn't know what that difficulty *looked* like. Some parents seemed to take to it like a duck to water while others struggled at every turn; I wanted to know what I was up against in hopes that I might figure out if I'd be the duck or if I'd be the one to drown.

When parents started talking, I bit my tongue and let them keep talking, and in many cases, they'd show more cards.

Sometimes it's the everyday things:

- "The work just never ends."
- "I don't know if I can handle another bedtime battle."
- "They never stop fighting except when they're asleep."

Other times, it's broader:

- "I feel like there isn't a *me* anymore. I'm just their mom/dad."
- "I don't know what I have less of these days—time or money. There's never enough of either."
- "I'm always worried about them. Even when they're right here. It's like I always have my anxiety dialed up to at least an 8."

I never got the impression they didn't love their kids or that they regretted having them, just that they were being honest about their situation. Many were just venting, because let's be real—parenting *is* hard, and we all need to vent about the tough things in our lives.

Interestingly, their attitudes shifted dramatically if I even hinted that I was having second thoughts about becoming a parent. This was especially true if I suggested that a person's comments about their experiences were making me rethink my future. Someone could be a breath away from saying, "If I had it to do over, I never would've had kids,"—or hell, in some cases they actually said it—but Lord, did that tune change when I said, "You know, I wonder if being a parent is for me after all." Then it was suddenly, "But kids are amazing!" and "It's all worth it in the end!"

I can't even blame them, to be honest. What I think happens when we show the "this is making me rethink having kids" card is that guilt catches up. It is incredibly taboo in our society to speak ill of anything relating to your kids. I think the sudden one-eighty from "parenting is the hardest thing ever!" to "but kids are the best!" is neither gaslighting nor cluelessness. I mean, it can be. Sometimes it definitely is. In general, though, I think it comes from the panicked realization that they've admitted to something they find deeply shameful, followed by the desperate need to save face.

This is especially evident when you consider the different reactions if they're alone with you versus in a group. No one wants other parents to hear them say, "You know what? You're smart. Skip this whole nightmare." I can't even blame them.

Get some people one-on-one, though, and the candor is eye-opening. My interaction with my coworker in chapter 9 was the first time a parent fully showed those cards—it was, after all, the first time I'd shown mine—but it wasn't the last. After talking to her, I started dipping my toes into that water with other people. Often with a wistful or even mournful sigh, they'd admit, "You're smart. I thought I knew what I was getting into, but..." or "Before I had my kids, I'd have tried to change your mind. Now that I have them, though, I say that if you're not absolutely 100% onboard... don't. You'll hate it." More than one said, "I never considered not doing it. It was what you do after you get married. It never occurred to me I could just... not."

None of them said they didn't love their kids. They just confessed that it was hard—a lot harder than they thought it would be—and that it really shouldn't be something someone "just does." Many expressed resentment that they were effectively brainwashed to believe parenting was compulsory; so much so that it was alien to them to imagine opting out without some earthshaking reason. I get that, you know? We live in a society where the default is to have kids. It often doesn't occur to people that we should opt *into* parenthood, not opt *out*. In other words, we all grow up believing that unless there's a good reason—a really, really damn good reason—not to have kids, then... you have kids.

To describe the epiphany some parents have in the context of this conversation, let me tell you a short side story. I promise, it relates.

While I was on Okinawa, I flew back to the States for something. One of the perks of living on the island was the Patriot Express. This was a military flight that went back to the U.S., and everyone stationed there—including dependents—was entitled to one round trip each year.

Not long after I returned, I was talking to someone else about my recent trip, and they mentioned they were going home soon themselves. They'd been gobsmacked by the price.

"I don't know how people can afford to go home as often as they do," they said. "It's so expensive!"

I said, "I took the Patriot Express. It's like $10."

"The *what?*"

I told them about the program. Somehow, in the chaos of transferring to the island, they'd missed that part of the orientation. (Not a big surprise; the orientation happens while you're completely *dis*oriented from jet lag and overwhelmed by the relocation. We all miss stuff at that stage.) They had no idea the Patriot Express was available to dependents.

You can probably imagine the look on their face when they realized they'd just bought a $1,000 non-refundable ticket when they could have taken the same trip for $10. That look and that feeling of, "Holy crap. Why didn't someone tell me *before* I made that investment?"

That's roughly the same reaction I saw in a number of parents when it sank in that they could've made a different choice. Not only had they been sold a package that didn't turn out anything like they were told it would, they'd assumed—because it was what they'd had shoved down their throats all their lives—that they *had* to buy it.

My friend still enjoyed their trip back to the U.S. They were just frustrated to realize they could've done things differently; that there was an option they'd missed that they would've jumped on.

Of course we all have to own our decisions. At the end of the day, we're responsible for informing ourselves and making our choices.

My argument here is simply that there is a lot of cultural resistance to making all of that information available. Parental regret is an enormous taboo. Expressing even the slightest frustration with parenthood leaves people—especially mothers—worried about being labeled bad parents. As such, the dialogue about struggling with parenthood or regretting it is severely limited, enough so that getting straight answers about *why* it's so hard can be like getting blood from a stone.

It's hard for parents to admit they're struggling unless it's couched in praise for how amazing parenthood really is—"It's the hardest job in the world, but there is nothing more amazing or rewarding!" It's hard for parents to admit they don't find every second of parenthood to be the epitome of bliss—"It's so, so hard, but I love everything about it!"

These days, there is more dialogue than there used to be. Social media has created a lot more opportunities to talk openly about things that used to be taboo, from menstruation to neurodivergence to, yes, how incredibly difficult it is to be a parent. More and more parents are speaking up about things they struggle with, things they wish they'd known going into it, and what they'd do differently. I would have sawed off a limb for that level of public discourse back when I was still trying to figure things out.

Some people don't like this. They don't think parents should be speaking on public platforms about anything but the positive sides of parenting. To be even a little bit negative is akin to telling their kids, "I wish you didn't exist."

I strongly disagree. In my opinion—and based on my experience and observations—it's important for people to be open and candid about their feelings and their regrets. I'm not saying anyone should be shouting from the rooftops that their kids were a mistake. It goes without saying that people should be mindful of their children's feelings. But there are ways to have honest conversations about parental regret without hurting kids. People should be able to say, "I don't enjoy being a parent" or express frustration that they were told it would be different without being accused of not loving their children.

Bottom line? Grown adults should be capable of nuance in both expressing and hearing such regrets without hurting kids' feelings or making knee jerk accusations at parents. If we could collectively develop this ability to have these conversations, I think more regretful parents would feel validated and seen, and more not-yet-parents would have adequate information to consider before choosing to have kids.

Everybody wins except people who think parenthood should be mandatory, and I'm perfectly happy with them losing.

CHAPTER 13

OLD ENOUGH TO GET PREGNANT

TOO YOUNG TO GET STERILIZED.

As we transitioned from infertile to childfree, our conversations shifted away from conception and on to the exact opposite subject: contraception.

People had been telling us for a long time, "When you give up, that's when it'll happen!" Because of course, that's all infertility is—we're just stressing too hard about it!

(As an aside... please don't say that to people. I don't care if you know someone who stopped trying and got pregnant five minutes later. Infertility sucks. It's painful. It's miserable. Cheerful platitudes like that really aren't helpful, and in fact, they hurt. Just. *Stop*.)

Anyway, while we'd hardly given up, we did take that platitude to heart as a dire warning: Now that we *don't* want it to happen, it probably will unless we're really, *really* careful.

This was where I ran headlong into an uncomfortable contradiction in our society. One I think I'd been vaguely aware of, but now couldn't avoid after experiencing both infertility and the childfree life. It's also impossible not to notice the deep-seated misogyny lying at its core.

At twenty-three, *no one* batted an eye at giving me fertility treatments. No one asked questions. No one tapped the brakes. I wanted a baby, and there wasn't a medical professional in my orbit who hesitated to help make that happen. Not. *One.*

At twenty-seven, I was far, far too young to be sterilized.

No one was shy about telling me that, either.

And yet, through four years of infertility, no one suggested I think twice about having the baby I now absolutely *did not want.*

No one said, "You might regret having kids someday."

No one said, "You still have plenty of time to decide if you want a baby."

No one said, "You'll change your mind."

Guess what, fam—I changed my mind.

And I'm not suggesting that people should say those things. It's intrusive and inappropriate unless you have a relationship with someone where your input is wanted or invited. The point is that people don't say the above, but they have zero problem letting their opinions be known about someone's choice to not have kids.

"You'll regret it someday when you're all alone!"

"You still have plenty of time, but don't wait too long or time will run out!"

"You'll change your mind."

By contrast, if someone has more kids than they can care

for, if they're already financially in dire straits, if their health is too fragile to withstand a pregnancy, if they're neglecting the kids they already have, if their relationship is volatile or unstable... it's still considered the height of rudeness to tell someone, "You really should think twice about having a baby."

To be clear, I'm not suggesting we *should* openly tell people what we think about them having a baby. I think it is rude and obnoxious to say any of that to someone. I simply think the same standard should apply when speaking to people who *don't* want to have a baby. It's inappropriate and rude to question someone's choice to have children. So why is it acceptable to openly question, criticize, and outright condemn someone's choice not to?

These double standards go beyond politeness, too, and on to the issue of bodily autonomy. It's a strange contradiction in our society that a woman is fully capable of making the unquestioned decision to become a mother, but that *same woman* is, *years later*, too young to decide *not* to become a mother.

And really, if we're going to make it all about regrets, let's be real: which decision is less reversible—sterilization, or a baby?

Many people insist that the only reason doctors hesitate to give tubals is that the procedure is more invasive than a vasectomy and also less reversible.

I call BS on that.

Yes, they are more invasive, and yes, they are harder to reverse, but that's not the conversation we have with our doctors. Oh, they'll bring that part up, but there's so, so many more layers that have nothing to do with the relative complexities of medical procedures.

Most of the time, it just keeps circling back to "You're too young" and "You'll change your mind." I've read and heard countless women describe this same thing, over and over and over, from doctors all over the U.S. and all over the world. It's sometimes dressed up in concern about risks and complications, but more often than not, it just keeps boiling down to women not being allowed to make a permanent decision to not have children.

Single women are even told by some doctors that their future husband might want a baby. Our ability to make reproductive decisions can literally be limited by the hypothetical desires of men *we haven't even met yet.*

As a bonus, some providers will still tell women that, by law, they must have their husband's written permission to get sterilized. At least in the United States, this is untrue. *A woman is not required **by law** to have her husband's permission to get sterilized.* Though with the way things are going, we'll see if that changes.

Men can and do run into difficulty trying to obtain a vasectomy, but in general, women have a much harder time getting sterilized than men. It is *so difficult* to get a tubal ligation as a childfree woman that people on Reddit have created a shared document listing providers in every U.S. state who *will* do it.

Long before that list was created, I decided I wanted to pursue a tubal ligation. I didn't want to waste time meeting doctors who wouldn't perform a tubal on a childfree woman, so I reached out to every OB/Gyn I could find in the state where I lived (Virginia). I emailed dozens and dozens of doctors, explaining that I was childfree and wanted to get a tubal ligation. I asked if this was an option for them.

Over the course of a couple of weeks, responses started trickling in.

One doctor said he would be willing to discuss it. *One.*

As luck would have it, he was fairly close to Norfolk, and he had appointments available.

I was still dubious when I showed up. A lifetime of medical trauma brings with it trust issues that don't go away overnight.

At first, it went reasonably well. I explained that I had thought it through, that I had been through some infertility and miscarriages, and that all of that had given us enough perspective to realize we didn't want children after all.

He wasn't as condescending or patronizing as a lot of doctors my childfree friends have encountered. He acknowledged that women could and did make the decision to not have kids.

But.

He wasn't comfortable sterilizing me.

So began a solid hour and a half of arguing with this man over my decision to be surgically sterilized.

His reasons for not wanting to do the procedure:

- "You could change your mind down the road and then sue me." (Couldn't the same be said for *any* elective medical procedure?)
- "You could have a serious reaction to the

anesthesia." (Does that stop you from performing other elective procedures?)

- "I could nick your aorta and you could bleed out." (...bruh.)

I asked if he was reluctant to help infertile women, since the resulting pregnancy carried far more significant risks than the tubal ligation procedure. He said that no one ever comes back to sue him because they had a baby after he treated them for infertility.

"But they sign the same waivers and releases that I would," I said. "So they have just as much of an ability to come back and sue you as someone who has a tubal."

"Sure, but no judge or jury is going to rule in their favor."

"No judge or jury is going to dismiss the fact that I'm an adult who signed a consent form either."

We were going in circles at this point, so he changed tactics. He tried to push me to get an IUD. I explained that synthetic hormones don't agree with me, and I was also concerned about some of the side effects that were being reported (especially since the IUD he was pushing was relatively new on the market). He was very enthusiastic about it and liked the results he was seeing. All of his patients so far were thrilled with it.

I was dubious because of the side effects, but it also hadn't escaped my notice that there were several advertisements for this specific IUD *prominently* displayed in his waiting room. In fact, I'd passed some of the time in the waiting room perusing the brochures, and though they were full of marketing language about being safe, effective, comfortable, etc., I still wasn't convinced. Pharmaceutical advertising has never sat well with me, especially since I've had at least two experiences in my life where a drug was similarly promoted in the waiting room, and then the doctor very eagerly encouraged me to try it.

So when this doctor has festooned his waiting room with glossy ads for a particular IUD, and then he's aggressively encouraging me to try that IUD despite my history with synthetic hormones and my concerns about safety issues...

...that's a little sus, am I right?

Then, he proposed a compromise: "You try a [brand name redacted] IUD for 6 months. If you still want the tubal after that time is up, then I'll do it."

I replied, "So in order to get the surgery that has risks you find unacceptable, I first have to spend six months with something that has risks *I* find unacceptable?"

He very confidently said that he was sure I would be fine with the IUD, and six months from now, I wouldn't want the tubal anymore. But I wasn't getting the tubal without a trial run with the IUD.

The IUD advertised all over his waiting room like it was God's gift to contraception.

Definitely sus.

But this was also the only doctor within my entire state who would even discuss a tubal with me. If he said no, then the answer was no.

For a hot minute, out of sheer frustration and resignation, I considered taking him up on the IUD. A lot of people got them and they seemed to be fine. Right?

My gut said *no*.

I thought it might be because I was just squicked out by the insertion/removal processes, and given how little trust I had in the phrase "you might feel a little cramping," I decided the anxiety alone was reason enough to listen to my gut. Ironically, in recent years, people have finally started to come forward and say that the insertion/removal processes are often *very* painful.

Things like this are why I trust my gut *way* more than I trust doctors.

Incidentally, I mentioned previously that I was diagnosed with Idiopathic Intracranial Hypertension in 2018. It's also referred to as Pseudotumor Cerebri because, as a neurologist explained it to me, the symptoms can mimic those of a brain tumor. It is, essentially, elevated cerebrospinal fluid pressure, and yeah, it's about as fun as it sounds.

I have been incredibly fortunate in that my case is relatively mild. While many patients have severe vision problems, debilitating headaches, and other issues, and many have to resort to brain surgery, my symptoms haven't been bad and have been controlled by a low dose of medication. I get some wicked headaches sometimes, especially when the weather changes (when the air pressure fluctuates), and I have some visual distortion, problems with eye strain, etc. It sucks, but it could be *a lot* worse.

Why am I randomly bringing this up?

Because a possible link has been established between the specific IUD that doctor was pushing on me and IIH. Many of the people in my online support group had this IUD and have significantly worse symptoms than I do. (Studies are currently ongoing to determine if there really is a causal link.)

There's no way to know for sure, but I shudder to imagine how much worse my IIH would be had I listened to that doctor about the IUD.

And again... people wonder why I have trust issues.

Not long after my attempts to pursue a tubal ligation, we moved to Okinawa. I broached the subject with a military doctor, but they made it pretty clear it wasn't going to happen.

We decided to try a different approach—see if Eddie could get a vasectomy.

This got some weird pushback from people we knew (not that we broadcasted it, but we did tell some people close to us). In those conversations, I heard an unsettling number of variations of, "What if something happens to you, he remarries, and he wants kids with his new wife?"

It was this really strange insinuation that we were doing this because *I* didn't want kids, not because *we* didn't want them. That he didn't want them with me, but after he replaced me, he might decide to have kids. Stranger still, there was never any implication that the reverse might be true— that if something happened to him and I remarried, I might want kids with husband 2.0.

No, it was just a lot of very serious concern about Eddie doing something for me that he might regret down the line when his next wife wanted kids.

Do y'all really think he was going to let a doctor put

needles and incisions in his nutsack for something he didn't want? Come on, now.

He made an appointment with a doctor on base, and we went in together. Given all the brick walls I'd beaten my head against in pursuit of my own sterilization, I was ready for a fight.

The conversation went like this:

Doctor: "Why do you want a vasectomy?"

Eddie: "Because I don't want kids."

Doctor: "Do you understand that this procedure should be considered irreversible[1]?"

Eddie: "That's exactly why I want it."

Doctor: "Sign here."

I'm pretty sure I did a Surprised Pikachu face at that point. That was it? No argument? No pushback? Seriously?

Yeah. Seriously. Eddie made an appointment, and a couple of weeks later... snippy snippy. It was that easy.

And like, I'm glad it was easy. I'm glad we didn't have to fight and argue for his right to make that choice for himself. I really, really am.

Still, I'd be lying if I said it didn't rankle that 23 year-old me was old enough to get fertility treatments, 27 year-old

Eddie was old enough to get a vasectomy, but 28 year-old me was "too young" and would "change [my] mind."

People continue to insist the issue is about the invasiveness and permanence of the tubal versus the vasectomy, but that has never been my experience at all. In all the years since then that I tried to get this procedure, the only time the invasiveness or risks have ever come into the conversation have been after I've already shot down the doctor's laundry list of reasons why I shouldn't get a tubal.

And eventually, when they truly run out of arguments, they just say, "Your husband has had a vasectomy, so you really don't need a tubal, do you?"

Now that I'm in my early forties and on the cusp of menopause—now that biology is close to making it a moot point anyway—I do have a doctor who's willing to do a bilateral salpingectomy. At this point, it's more about cancer prevention (since the procedure can lower the risk of ovarian cancer), but I'll take it.

It just would've been nice to have as much autonomy to prevent pregnancy as I'd had to encourage one.

CHAPTER 14

OUT OF STEP

BEING CHILDFREE IN THE MILITARY

Though I grew up adjacent to the military, I wasn't really part of the military community before I got married. We occasionally went to the commissary or the Exchange, and I think I've literally set foot on more ships than my Sailor husband, but I never lived on base until I moved to Okinawa.

That was also my first exposure to one of the subcultures in the military: milspouses. In particular, military wives. There were husbands, too, but it was mostly wives, especially in the groups (which I believe have mostly shifted to calling themselves spouses' groups instead of wives' groups, but at the time, it was wives').

I knew from the start that I would never really find a place within that community. My first attempt to join an enlisted wives' group was shortly after Eddie was deployed. I was barely a month into being married, living away from home for the first time, and suddenly my husband was gone indefinitely. While I still had my family and friends reasonably close by, and I was working so much I didn't have a lot of free time, I wanted to find some community among the spouses of my husband's shipmates. I was still finding my footing in the world of an active duty spouse, and I'd always heard the wives' groups were a good place for support and friendship.

Not long after the deployment kicked off, there was an event for dependents. There were booths set up for people to get information about TriCare (military health insurance), on-base activities and facilities, and—in this case—the enlisted wives' group for the ship my husband was attached to.

I approached the organizer of the group and said I was newly married. It was quickly apparent that... she wasn't interested. She engaged with a pasted-on smile, nodded a little as I spoke, and kept glancing over my shoulder until she finally saw someone she knew. At that point, she abruptly excused herself from the conversation and went to talk to the other person.

Well, okay. Message received.

Fine. As I said, I still had people living close by. I was very fortunate; being far, far from home is part of military life.

A year later, in early 2004, we were in Norfolk, but I didn't pursue any connection with the wives' groups. I joined an online group run by the ombudsmen—a few spouses who acted as liaisons between the ship and the families back home during deployments—just so I could get updates, but I made no effort to socialize. Once bitten, and all that. Fine. I made friends at work and had others through the model horse hobby.

2008 was the year we made the decision to be childfree. It was also the year we transferred to Okinawa.

An overseas PCS is when the isolation of the military life really makes itself known. Our families and friends were suddenly an ocean away, and the military community became the only community we had.

I was still gun shy about the enlisted wives' groups. I honestly don't remember if I made any attempt to join them. It's been almost 16 years since I moved there, and I don't recall any interactions with any formal or informal groups. Either way, I didn't join any of the groups during my three years there.

Fortunately, I didn't really need them, as most of my social life for the first year or so was online. I was actively involved in an online writing forum with thousands of members, I blogged frequently about our adventures on the island, and social media was becoming a thing. Yes, I'm aging myself—this was the early, early years of Facebook, and it became a lifeline between us and our people back home.

There did come a point when I was itching for in-person interaction. I spent many, many hours writing, and we also spent a lot of time exploring the island, but for the most part, it was just us.

Eddie and I lived on Camp McTureous, which consisted of an elementary school, a chapel, a Shoppette (like a small convenience store), and housing. Nothing else. We had no use for the school or the chapel, so we didn't go to either of those.

We struggled to connect with people around us, too. Most of our neighbors had kids. The socializing among wives in housing centered around their kids. Even activities that didn't focus on kids became a venue for moms to talk about mom things.

Our other opportunity to socialize was among the people Eddie worked with. We did hang out with them, but it was challenging to find a lot of common ground. They were either single guys who liked to party, or married with kids.

Within the military community, there is simply not a lot of room for people who don't want to party and aren't interested in kids. We found ourselves at the edges of many groups —hanging out and socializing, but never quite feeling like part of the group.

We did, fortunately, make some friends over there. Two other couples without kids also enjoyed exploring the island, trying new restaurants, and snorkeling. I also met a mom who found my blog before coming to Okinawa, and we would often hang out or go exploring. So we weren't completely isolated or lonely. We made friends (and in fact we're still friends with them now, over a decade after we left the island).

The difficulty came in finding a place within the broader military community. Most commands would have holiday parties and other gatherings throughout the year, and especially the more casual parties would often self-segregate as the event went on. The wives would gravitate toward one area. The husbands toward another.

Early on, I tried to hang out with the wives, but the conversations skewed heavily toward pregnancy and kids. There's nothing wrong with this—it was an important part of their lives, and it was something they all had in common. Of course they were going to talk about it. Stick half a dozen writers in a room, we're going to talk about writing. If it's half a dozen moms... well. What do we expect? It was perfectly understandable and reasonable; it just wasn't something I could relate to or really take part in.

So, I'd end up moving to where the guys were hanging out. Oftentimes this meant listening to them talk shop, because my God, none of them could leave work at work, but it was at least more interesting than placentas or potty training.

Time and again, I'd come home from these events relieved that I could finally return to my own social circle, even if that was 99% online. I joked that being a writer was turning me into a recluse, and to some extent that was true—I was a *serious* workaholic—but it was also a by-product of not being able to connect with many people in my real world. My small handful of friends, yes—I will always be grateful for them—but feeling like the odd man out in a room full of people has never been a comfortable feeling.

A lot of people felt isolated because they lived on a tiny island somewhere in the Pacific.

For me, there was nothing more isolating than being a childfree woman in the military community.

When I got to Spain in 2015, I wanted to do things differently. I didn't want to spend another few years having little to no social interaction outside of the internet and my husband. I did have friends in Europe who I planned to visit and who visited me, and a handful from the U.S. came to visit as well. I wanted local friends, though.

This time, I decided to be more proactive. I'd given up on enlisted wives' groups, but there was a thriving Facebook community where service members and dependents could connect and share information. On a whim, I pitched a writing group to see if there was anyone interested in hanging out and talking about writing. To my surprise, there was a pretty big turnout from the start, and I ended up making friends with a few members. Two in particular became good friends, and both were moms. One was especially happy to have a non-mom friend because she liked being able to talk to someone about her interests and her career.

To paraphrase a comment she made one day: "The most frustrating part of being a milspouse is that I'm defined as his wife, then their mom, and maybe—eventually, if we have time —myself. More people want to talk to me about my husband's career than about mine."

I could totally relate. We bonded over having ambitions outside of being a milspouse or a mom, and talking about things besides the Navy.

Ironically, I'd been told for years that there was a huge divide between enlisted wives and officers' wives. That the latter looked down on the former, that the former thought the latter were snobs, you name it. Yet here we were, an enlisted wife and an officer's wife, not giving a single damn about our husbands' ranks or jobs because there were way more interesting things to talk about.

So while I did maintain my reclusive lifestyle to some extent in Spain, I made more of an effort to find people this time, and I succeeded. I also traveled more and saw a lot of my friends who were scattered around Europe. The four years in Spain were probably a lot better for my mental health than the three on Okinawa, at least in terms of socializing.

Larger group events were still a struggle for me. The guys

wanted to drink and talk about work. The women wanted to talk about babies.

Again, they weren't doing anything wrong. They had something in common that they wanted to talk about. And none of it made me regret my choices. I simply didn't vibe with them because we had vastly different experiences and interests.

It was just hard sometimes to be that woman at the table who didn't drink, didn't work with the guys, and didn't want or have kids.

And sometimes, it wasn't just the lack of something in common. Sometimes, upon learning that I not only didn't have kids, I didn't *want* them, people couldn't *quite* hide their distaste. The little wrinkle of the nose. The side-eye. The way they pointedly didn't even bother making small talk with me at future events. The backhanded remarks about how deployments must be a *breeze* for someone who doesn't have to be a single parent.

These reactions aren't exclusive to milspouses, of course. I've had that reaction from other people, and some have been anything but subtle about it. Being childfree is still alien to many, and some don't quite know how to react to it. And some do react negatively to it for any number of reasons. That was something I learned to live with very, very early on.

It just hits harder when you're in a small, insular community, largely isolated from everyone *but* that community, for years at a stretch.

CHAPTER 15

JUST THE TWO OF US

WEATHERING LIFE'S STORMS

Sixteen years have gone by since Eddie and I made the decision to be childfree, and a lot of life happens in that much time.

Between 2008 and 2024, we have moved five times. Four of those were across oceans. Anyone who's moved knows it's a headache and a half, and it can put a strain on any relationship. Add in transcontinental road trips and transoceanic relocations, and the stress is off the charts.

Somehow, other military families navigate these with children in tow. My hat is off to them because just getting my cats across the U.S. and then into Japan was more than enough for me. Can it be done with kids? Absolutely. Can *I* handle it with kids? Well, fortunately I don't have to find out, but I'm pretty sure the answer is no.

That's been a common theme throughout the last decade and a half. It was in the years leading up to the decision to be childfree, too. Whenever something happened or we were faced with something stressful, there was that constant drumbeat of "How much harder would this be if we had kids?"

In the infertility days, I brushed that off. Obviously people could handle it.

But over time, I've been more honest with myself. People can handle it, yes. But would I want to? Is that the life I want?

No. It isn't. And that's okay. I like how my life has turned out, and some of the hard times have underscored the fact that I made the right decision with regard to children.

Over the years, Eddie and I have weathered marital struggles, including briefly brushing up against divorce twice. The first was while we were on Okinawa. It isn't really important why; there was no infidelity or anything. It was just one of those periods where we were far enough out of alignment that we were unhappy.

We were also living overseas, which meant moving back to the U.S.—together or separately—was extraordinarily complicated. It was, however, far less complicated without kids. We never felt like we were chained to each other or like we *had* to make it work. There was no pressure to work it out for the kids, so we worked it out for ourselves. When we again hit a rough patch while we lived in Nebraska, same deal.

In the end, we obviously worked it out. I don't know how it would have played out had there been kids involved. I'm just glad that wasn't something we had to consider while we were resolving things.

In 2022, shortly after we moved to Pittsburgh, I had to have major oral surgery. It needed to happen quickly because there was a serious infection that could potentially spread. It also wasn't covered by insurance and had to be paid for out of pocket and upfront. All $55,000 of it. No, that's not a typo. Between credit cards, a loan, and some liquidated investments, we were able to cover it.

Then there was the recovery time. For ten days, I was basically useless. I was in a ton of pain, and my days were divided into random intervals of sleeping, staring at the TV, trying to eat, and taking hot showers. The showers were one of the only things that brought relief (painkillers and such don't do much for me), and I would sometimes get up at 2 or 3 in the morning just to let hot water beat on my sore face.

During that time, my husband took care of me in between working (he worked at home). He'd cook, bring me icepacks, and drive me to the surgeon's office for follow-ups. Everyone I worked with (co-authors, audiobook narrators, editors, translators, etc.), not to mention my readers, were infinitely patient with me; they all insisted that I prioritize recovering over anything else. Literally all I had to do for a solid week and a half was rest and recover. No one made any demands of me except my cats, and all they wanted was snacks and cuddles.

After the first ten days, I was more or less functional. My sleep pattern became more normal (as normal as my sleep pattern ever is), and I steadily started working again. There was still pain, but it wasn't so bad. Having that much time to just recover and do nothing else was a godsend.

This is partly a result of being self-employed with the flexibility to take time off; a day job with limited PTO would've demanded a much faster recovery. I vividly remember how hard it was to return to work too soon following my miscarriage, and there was far less physical pain involved. Going back to work after just a handful of days this time? That would've been hell. And it's definitely a reality, too; my surgeon said most of his patients return to work after "about five days." After I'd recovered, I asked someone at the clinic, "Is that five-day turnaround because they're actually feeling better? Or is it because they can't take more time off work?" No one really had an answer, but I think I can guess.

So I didn't have the pressure to return to work, and I also didn't have to take care of small people. There was no guilt over not doing enough for the kids, or extra pain and exhaustion from pushing myself too hard.

Could I have recovered from the surgery with kids? Of course.

Am I unwaveringly glad I didn't have to? You better believe it.

Of course none of these are things that parents cannot get through. For us, though, these difficult seasons have never come and gone without one or both of us saying, at some point, "I am *so glad* we don't have kids."

That's not out of glibness or smugness; it's simply an expression of how overwhelmed we are by a situation and how much *more* overwhelmed we would be if we were also caring for children. For us, it's affirmation that we made the right decision. That we understood ourselves, and how much we could and wanted to handle.

Everyone has to figure out their own path, which includes figuring out what they *can* handle in their lives, and what they *want* to handle in their lives.

Obviously we're dealt some cards whether we want them or not. Health issues. Natural disasters. Family crises. Financial difficulties. Job changes. Things happen in life, and we simply have to roll with them.

But there are other cards we can accept or decline.

We can choose to get married. Stay single. Cohabitate. Be poly. Buy a place with some friends and rock it like the *Golden Girls*. Society certainly has opinions about which of those options are acceptable and which are non-negotiable, but at the end of the day, most of us at least have some choice in the matter.

The same goes for having children.

There are, of course, situations where people have their choices taken away, whether that choice is to opt in *or* out of parenthood. I'm not discounting those or pretending they don't exist. They absolutely do.

For those of us outside of those situations, though, children *are* optional. You can have one. You can have eight. You can adopt, foster, have biological kids, or do all three.

You can also say... "Children are not for me." You can look at everything that parenthood entails, both the good and the bad, and decide that you don't want to sign up for the package deal.

Will you miss out on things? Of course. Whatever choice you make, you're going to miss out on things. It's just a matter of deciding which things you don't want to live without, and what you're willing to take on in order to experience those things.

Some people don't want to miss out on being a parent, and the price of admission—the downsides to having kids—is one they're willing to pay.

For others, the downsides to having kids aren't something

they're willing to accept, and the price of admission—missing out on the good things—is fine with them.

In my case, I don't find myself longing for any of the things that come with parenthood. I've had the odd flicker of envy now and then for some of the highlight moments, but these are fleeting. I sometimes momentarily envy Olympic athletes, too, but that doesn't mean I want to turn my whole life upside down to pursue those gleaming highlights.

What I've longed for more than anything is a quiet life with the freedom to do things on a whim. I want peace that isn't compatible with the constant anxiety and vigilance of having a child.

More than any other time, it is the chaotic and tumultuous periods that underscore how much I want that peaceful, flexible life, and how much I have exactly that. It drives home that while my life is far from perfect, it's as close to perfect as I can realistically expect it to be.

Through the difficult times especially, I look back on that decision I made back in 2008. I see the butterfly effect it had on my world.

And I wouldn't change a thing.

CHAPTER 16

ALL THESE YEARS LATER
CHILDFREE AFTER 40

This meandering story brings me to now. As I write this, it's mid 2024. My husband recently turned 43. I'll be 44 in a few months.

Had things played out differently, the baby we lost in 2006 would have turned 17 this May, not long after Eddie's birthday.

Like I do every year, I paused around that time and thought about what might have been. I thought about where we'd be. What life would look like.

It isn't regret or even nostalgia. It isn't a desire to go back and do things differently. Rather, I imagine what that could've been, and I feel a renewed sense of contentedness. A sense that while I couldn't have known it at the time, the wind had thrown me in the right direction. The river changed course, and we made choices and chose directions from that new course instead of trying to reclaim the old one.

That river led us to who and where we are now. In the

years since we chose to be childfree, we've *lived*. We've traveled extensively. All told, we spent seven years living abroad. My career has gone places I never imagined, and I found more fulfilment and satisfaction in my work than I ever thought possible. That career has also brought people into my life who I deeply cherish—friends from all over the world.

Would I have traveled and made friends and lived with kids? Of course. But it would be different. There are people in my world with whom I never would've crossed paths. There are experiences that never would've crossed my mind.

In 2009, I went to my ten-year high school reunion. Ten years later, I went to my twenty-year. Many of my classmates had spouses and kids in 2009, and I'd say the vast majority did by 2019, so a lot of catching up involved talking about their families as well as our careers.

At the ten-year reunion, my first book would be released a few weeks later. It still remained to be seen if this would be a career or just a thing I checked off my bucket list. I still had no idea how my future looked, both as a person and as an author, but I could say that I had accomplished the goal of writing and publishing a book.

At the twenty-year, I was over a hundred books deep into my career. I was making a solid living, still loving every minute of it, and wouldn't trade a thing.

My classmates with kids were happy with their lives. I was that classmate who'd traveled all over the place, had a career I was super proud of, and had skipped having kids, and I was happy with my life, too.

There was also a book someone had saved from our graduation year where we'd all written predictions about what our lives would look like after high school.

Twenty years earlier, my 18 year-old self had written:

"Take six months off, go to the University of Washington (either English or political science), probably become a writer. Maybe get married someday, no kids. Maybe get another tattoo."

That six months turned into almost twenty years (I'm finishing up that degree now at a different university!), but the rest? Right on the money. Became a writer. Got married. No kids. Got... well, I had one tattoo when I graduated high school and I have fourteen now, so if anything, I underestimated a little in that department.

The point, though, is that on the cusp of forty, I was a version of myself that even my senior-in-high-school self could envision. Back then, I didn't see motherhood in my future. All these years later, after a period of wanting kids and struggling with infertility, it turns out that I knew myself all along after all. I'm a vastly different person from that kid, but I'm also very much the same.

But all these years later, I still go back to those infertility years every May and every October, and I think about what might have been. I revisit the crossroads and imagine where we might've gone and who we might've become had we chosen the other direction.

And each time, I come away with a deep sense of peace.

The life I have now is far from perfect—no one's life is perfect—but there is nothing missing that would be fulfilled by motherhood. There is no pang of regret or pull to course correct and go back in the direction I chose not to go back then.

More and more over the years, I realize that while I probably would've been a good mother—I certainly would've *tried* to be—I wouldn't have been a happy one. The trappings of motherhood were not and are not for me. I would've been the mother who's counting down until her kids move out and she can have her life back.

That isn't the way I wanted to live back then, and it isn't the way I want to live now. Is that selfish? Sure. But I don't think it's a bad thing to acknowledge that my particular flavor of selfishness isn't compatible with motherhood. It certainly isn't healthy for kids. The only thing I want to have less than kids is kids who are resented or regretted. That's not fair to them.

I'll be honest: there *are* times when I stop and ask myself if it was a mistake. If we're missing out, especially as we watch our peers post photos of their kids' graduations and such. But those times are fleeting; I quickly remember what else parenthood entails beyond milestones and Kodak moments, and I remember what my life has been like over the past decade and a half.

I have never—not once—asked myself if it was a mistake and answered *yes*. The answer has always been a resounding *no*.

But the fact that I'm even questioning it means I'm not sure, right?

No, it doesn't. I question everything I do, even when I'm sure about them. It isn't so much second-guessing myself as it is checking in.

Maybe it's an after effect of sticking with the infertility struggle for as long as I did. I didn't give myself the space I truly needed to question what I was doing. I was so committed and so afraid of losing my husband or being seen as a failure that I put on blinders and kept pushing forward.

When I look back and realize how vastly different my life could've been had biology cooperated during that four years, it spooks me. It genuinely gives me that almost-a-car-crash, just-dodged-a-bullet feeling. What if I'd gotten pregnant during that eighteen months or so where I was far less sure than I was willing to admit?

Since then, I've had a habit of checking in with myself about things. Even when a ship has well and truly sailed, I'll still reevaluate how I feel.

And time and time again, when I check in about my decision to be childfree, I find nothing but peace.

To reiterate, because it really is what this all boils down to:

There is nothing missing from my life that would be fulfilled by motherhood

---

As I write this section, it's early June, so shortly after the would-be birthday of the baby we lost. I did my usual "what if things had been different?", but something occurred to me that never has before. For as visual as I am—for as clearly and vividly as I can imagine things—I have never been able to conjure up what that child might've looked like. That bothered me a little in the beginning, mostly because it was so incongruous with the way my mind usually works, but it doesn't now.

Looking back, I have to wonder if some part of me knew that there wasn't a child to envision. There never would be. The image I conjure is abstract and nebulous, and truly, so was my relatively short-lived dream of being a mother. While I was fiercely determined to have a baby during that time, I think... on some level... I knew.

Earlier, I mentioned how I would imagine my life after my job in Norfolk, and how I'd envision being a writer. I saw it so much more clearly than I ever saw my future as a mother. Maybe not the same genre, maybe not with quite so many books, but the image of myself as a writer was so vivid, it was almost tangible.

The life I have now? *That's* what I envisioned. It's even better than I thought it would be, too. The money is better. The job is amazing. I'm surrounded by incredible colleagues. I've met dozens upon dozens of people I would've otherwise missed out on.

As I've said, there is nothing I've done in my life that a parent couldn't have done. Many of my friends and colleagues in this industry are parents, and they're happy and thriving. But I know myself, and I know that *I* could not have done them while also balancing parenthood. The sleep deprivation alone would have dashed a lot of dreams, as would the financial pressures.

I know myself.

I always, always, always dreamed about being a writer. Not a mother. I saw a future with kids just because that's what people did, then found out being childfree was an option. Changed my mind when I got married, but even then, it was only about being a mom/having a baby for a year or so. After that, it was just about the infertility being *over*. When I was frustrated at my job or just unhappy, I dreamed about the life I have now: writing for a living. Not being a mom.

Another thing I've observed about myself is that I don't think I have the patience to be a good parent. Right now, I have a young cat. He's about two years old, and he is still doing a lot of things that kittens do. He gets into things. He knocks things over. He tries to climb where he doesn't belong. We have to put childproof latches on our cabinets, or else he'll evict all of the cans and jars onto the kitchen floor (yeah, he's weird even by cat standards).

Jason: "Who, me??"

Like most cats, though, these shenanigans come in pretty short bursts. He'll be driving me bonkers, and five minutes later, he's out cold for a good hour.

Still, it's not at all unusual for me to text Eddie (who works upstairs) with, *Come get the kid, please.* The cat's mischief rarely lasts longer than ten or fifteen minutes, but my patience can run out well before that point.

So imagine if, instead of a young cat, I were dealing with a child instead. They'll run out of steam eventually, too, but if my patience can't outlast my cat's energy bursts, is it really going to outlast a kid's? Especially if I'm also sleep-deprived on top of it?

If reasonably well-rested me can hit the wall with a cat getting into things, then the version of me running on fumes isn't going to make it through an entire day with a small child. There's no way around that. I don't care if "it's different when they're yours." It's different because you don't have a *choice* when they're yours.

If I'm being honest with myself—truly and brutally honest—I don't think it would be different *enough* with my own kids. I think I would be miserable, and as a result, they would be miserable too. That's not fair to anyone.

So, I didn't have kids. We made the decision, made the leap, and embarked wholeheartedly into being childfree.

The life I ended up living...

The person I ended up being...

This is who I was always meant to be.

CHAPTER 17

BINGO!

Childfree people hear a lot of the same comments over and over and over again. It happens so frequently, we refer to it as being bingoed, since we could literally create BINGO cards with these ridiculous remarks.

Sometimes they're well-meaning. Honestly, they're probably said with good intentions most of the time. The concept of being childfree is alien to a lot of people, and they can't imagine just... not having kids.

Sometimes the remarks are not so well-intentioned. Recently, I've seen a lot of TikTok and YouTube videos calling out (in particular) men who criticize childfree women, especially those who choose not to get married. The targets of these videos are incredibly negative and even mean-spirited, describing childfree women in nasty, vitriolic ways that don't need to be repeated here. As if there is something grotesquely wrong with someone who lacks the desire to become a parent, and it's tenfold more grotesque if that someone is a woman.

And to be frank, even when comments *are* well-meaning, they're more often than not inappropriate, intrusive, and presumptuous. The reason I want to break them down in this chapter is two-pronged:

1. To explain to people who say them why these comments are—regardless of intent—misguided and inappropriate.
2. To help childfree people—especially younger people—see that they are not alone, that they are within their rights to push back against these remarks, and to hopefully offer some ways to articulate their responses.

I want to address some of them through the lens of someone who's been on both ends of the spectrum—from desperately wanting a baby to vehemently childfree. I'm also on the cusp of menopause, so I know what's like to be young and infertile, young and childfree, and childfree with the biological clock rapidly ticking down. Though to be honest I wish that clock would tick down a little faster—omg, mother nature, *hurry up*—but I digress.

Basically, I'm at the point where the motherhood ship (the mothership?) has pretty much sailed. I'm no longer a twentysomething who people will talk down to and insist I'm too young to know who I am or what I want. So let's go over some of the popular things people say to the childfree, and how those look in the rearview of fortysomething. And yes, I'm gonna get a little spicy in this chapter, because that's what happens when you've heard this stuff over and over and over for years.

"WHO WILL TAKE CARE OF YOU WHEN YOU'RE OLD?"

I don't know about y'all, but I live 2,500 miles away from my parents. Are your children going to stay geographically close enough to take care of you? What is your backup plan if their lives take them to the other side of the world during your elder years?

Even if you do live close to your parents, do you have the resources to provide round-the-clock care to an elderly person? Do you have a job? Children who also require your care? Are you in a position to be a parent's primary caregiver? Some people are. Many are not. Some people are able to devote months or years to caring for an ailing parent. Some cannot, even if they want to.

And let's be honest: some people don't want to. Some are not mentally, emotionally, physically, or financially equipped, and some people just... don't want to take on that role. Maybe they're estranged from their parents. Maybe they're barely coping with whatever is already on their plate. There are any number of reasons why someone cannot or will not take care of their elderly parents, and as economic conditions worsen and people's resources are stretched thinner, it's going to become less and less feasible to bank on your kids taking care of you in your twilight years.

It isn't fair or realistic to have children for the purpose of making sure you are taken care of when you're elderly. It's also a sad fact that not every child outlives their parents. Of course this is a devastating experience that no one foresees or desires, but it is the unfortunate reality for some. So if the only reason someone chooses to have a kid is so they're taken care of at the end of their life, that may not even pan out.

Bottom line? Having kids does not guarantee someone will take care of you when you're old. It's also incredibly presumptuous and, I would venture, cruel to have a child as insurance for elder care or for someone to come visit you in the old folks' home. To create a brand new human being and automatically place on their shoulders the burden of your elder care is...

...what's that word people always use to describe the childfree?

Oh.

Right.

Selfish.

"YOU'LL NEVER KNOW LOVE/ TRUE LOVE/ UNCONDITIONAL LOVE UNTIL YOU HAVE A CHILD."

This is as insulting as it is nonsense. It's also dangerous: if it turns out the parent doesn't feel that love and is going to be one of countless parents who abuses their kids, are you going to adopt the child? Or take responsibility for pressuring them into having kids they didn't want?

Stop it. I can fully respect that the love you have for your kids is like no other love you've ever experienced, and that's completely valid. But don't weaponize that into FOMO to shame someone into having kids.

Look, love for everyone is different. You feel different love for your parents, your siblings, and your friends. Does an only child not know love because they don't know what it's like to love a sibling? Of course not.

Also, as I've mentioned before, a parent once explained to me that the love you have for your child isn't just hearts and sunshine. It's a deep, intense worry. It's protectiveness. It's fear.

It is love, of course, and for many, it's amazing. But it's also deeply stressful.

My husband and I already have a lot of anxiety. We don't wish to sign up for that particular system upgrade. We're good.

"THERE ARE A LOT OF INFERTILE PEOPLE OUT THERE WHO WOULD GIVE ANYTHING TO HAVE THE BABY YOU DON'T WANT!"

This is one that will instantly raise my hackles and get my teeth gnashing every time. As someone with firsthand experience of the hell that is infertility? Don't you *dare* use me or my struggle to emotionally manipulate someone into having children. Don't you dare. Even while I was neck deep in that struggle, I *loathed* my experience being used to strong arm people into becoming parents. It's cruel, manipulative, exploitative, and just plain wrong.

I am not your martyr. I am not your emotional leverage.

Would you tell someone who chooses not to run marathons that there are people who'd give anything just to be able to walk? I certainly hope not. So why would you emotionally blackmail people into parenthood?

If you're a childfree or on-the-fence person, and someone feeds you this garbage, you have my permission—as someone who's *been* the infertile person they're referencing—to tell them to pound sand, and you don't have to be polite about it. Manipulation and cruelty aren't polite, so I hereby bless you with carte blanche to *match that energy*.

"IT'S DIFFERENT WHEN THEY'RE YOUR OWN."

Is it, though? Is it really?

And what happens if it's not? What happens if the person takes you at your word, has children, and discovers that—surprise!—it isn't actually different? Are you going to adopt those kids? Because it isn't like they can be sent back. There are no returns or take-backsies.

Also, quite frankly, I think this kind of gaslighting nonsense leads to abuse. To be clear, I'm not absolving abusive parents for their abuse. It's 100% their responsibility. But when you convince a person who doesn't want or like kids to have them because "it'll be different when their yours," and then it turns out it's not, and that parent takes it out on those kids...

Yeah, it's firmly the parents' responsibility, but I can't help but wonder how much abuse and neglect would be prevented if we listened to people when they said, "I don't like kids and I don't want them." Because knowing how much child abuse exists, why would you encourage someone who doesn't want them to have them?

That's not to say every abuser—or even most abusers—were people who didn't want kids but caved. I have personally known some people who absolutely wanted their kids and then abused them. Some of them insist they love them despite mountains of evidence to the contrary.

Nevertheless, the bait-and-switch "it's different when they're yours!" can certainly lay the groundwork for miserable, toxic, and even abusive situations. When someone is pressured into having kids, and they find themselves trapped in a life they hate and can't escape, that's not healthy. Not for the parents, and absolutely not for the kids.

If only for the sake of the kids, don't pressure people who don't want them into having them.

"THERE'S MORE TO LIFE THAN PARTYING!"

This is another one that really grinds my gears. It drives me utterly bats how many people think that you either have kids, or you drink and party. There is no in between.

Y'all, I *hate* partying. I don't drink. I don't like being around drunk people (especially since, being the one who doesn't drink, I *always* end up being designated driver *and* designated babysitter). Clubs are loud and overstimulating. That's not 43-year-old me talking. I went to a few clubs after I turned 21, but it was never my scene. I just don't enjoy it. Neither does Eddie.

For some reason, though, the only existence people can imagine for the childfree is one of utter hedonism.

What does childfree life look like? Well, for us, it's pretty quiet most of the time. Eddie and I are mostly homebodies. We have hobbies that we partake in at home. We spend our evenings hanging out in the living room with the cats, or we might go out to dinner and hit up some hobby-related stores. Not gonna lie—one of the biggest perks of having season tickets for hockey is that it forces us to get out of the house and *not* be at home all the time.

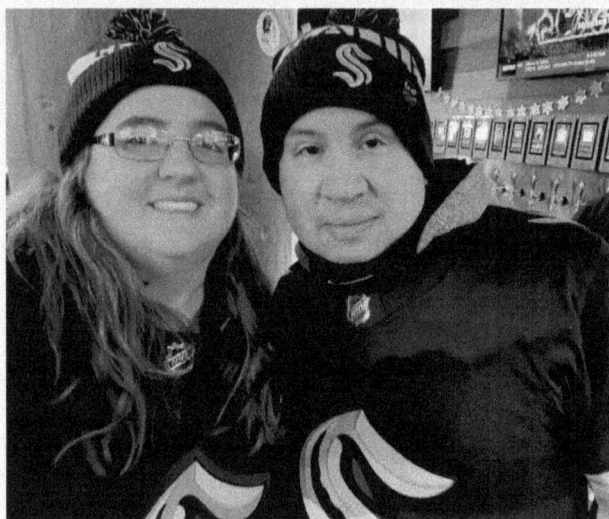

Shh. Don't tell the Penguins that we're Kraken fans too...

That's not to say we're complete hermits. We can easily stay home for days at a time, and hockey is a good excuse to keep us from holing up for a week or more. But we also like to travel sometimes, either on elaborately planned trips or spur of the moment jaunts.

Once in a while, we'll get in the car and take off somewhere. There was a Saturday not long after we moved to Pittsburgh where we grabbed our cameras and took off, and the next thing we knew, we were at Niagara Falls. Another weekend, we took off to Binghamton, New York, after a hockey game so we could go to the zoo and see their Pallas's Cat kittens (100% worth it, 10/10 would recommend).

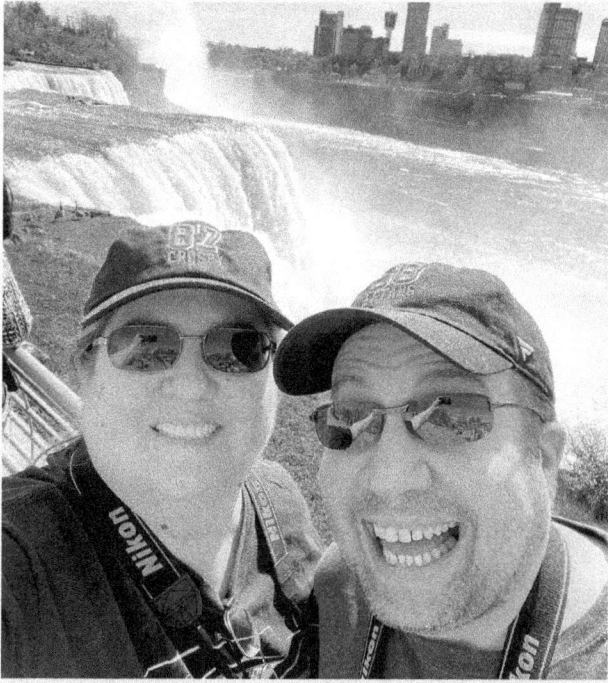

Random road trip to Niagara Falls!

When we lived in Spain, I lamented to Eddie over dinner one night that I was working on a book set in modern day Rome, but I couldn't remember the vibe of Rome. We'd been there a year earlier, but I just couldn't quite get there in my head. He looked at me and said, "I have a four-day weekend."

That was Monday. We flew out on Thursday and spent four amazing days in Rome.

That's the wild childfree life for us—the pleasantly boring homebody life punctuated by hockey games and occasional trips to wherever.

There's no running around to soccer practice or music lessons. There's no spending hours a night helping with homework and then trying to persuade everyone to go to bed. There's none of the constant noise and activity that comes with having kids in the house.

For some people, that life would be miserable and dull. That's fine. It's not for everyone, but it's absolutely for us. The life of a parent sounds like a nightmare for us, so we just... don't do it.

We have a life that involves jobs, hobbies, and travel. Some people do party, and that's perfectly valid. To me, that's about as appealing as being a parent—neither version is wrong or bad, they're just not what I want, same as the parent or the partier wouldn't want to live like I do.

So can we please stop with this idea that the only *possible* existence outside of parenthood is nonstop partying?

YOU'D BE A GREAT PARENT.

Maybe. But I sure wouldn't be a happy one. Is that selfish? Prioritizing my own happiness over making the sacrifices that come with being a parent? Maybe. Probably. But I don't think that's necessarily a bad thing. If I'm that selfish, am I really someone who should be raising a child? Probably not.

IT'S WHAT WOMEN ARE SUPPOSED TO DO.

No, it's what you've decided I'm supposed to do. I have (at least for now) autonomy over my life and (in some states) my body. The only thing I'm "supposed" to do is pay taxes and die. Whatever I do in between is my business.

Also, the *only* other person on the planet who gets *any* say in my reproductive decisions is my husband, and even then, he's not deciding if I do or don't have kids. He's making absolutely zero decisions about what I'm "supposed" to do. He's making a decision about what *he* wants to do. I make a decision about what I want to do. Then we as a couple decide what we're going to do—have kids together, don't have kids together, or move on separately so we can find more compatible partners.

Nobody else gets to make those decisions. Nobody else gets to assert their values and morals on me, my marriage, my body, or my life.

If someone's giving you this particular BINGO square of nonsense, just remember that they don't have any authority over you. They aren't affected one way or another by your choice—only you, your partner, and your hypothetical children are affected by it. This person has no dog in the race except trying to make *you* comply with *their* values.

You're not going to convince them of this, of course. People who believe in gender roles like that tend to believe in them very strongly, and they can sometimes get downright hostile toward people who reject those roles. Don't waste your energy beating your head against their brick wall of bullshit. Just keep reminding yourself it's a *them* problem, not a *you* problem.

If you go on about your merry childfree way and they don't like it?

Let 'em die mad about it.

LIFE IS POINTLESS WITHOUT KIDS.

It's not fair to bring kids into the world solely to give yourself purpose. That's selfish. If you want to be a parent, then by all means, knock yourself out. But you're creating a whole human being. One who will have to grow up and find their way in this unforgiving world. Putting the pressure on them to provide purpose and meaning in your life is just selfish and unfair.

WHAT ABOUT THE FAMILY NAME?

I don't know, man. I just don't see how it's beneficial to the kid to exist for the purpose of carrying on a name. Especially since there is then pressure on them to also have kids and keep the name going. To what end, you know? When do people just get to exist as themselves instead of vessels for a name?

YOUR PARENTS DESERVE GRANDCHILDREN.

Sure. But my parents also understand that their grandchildren would be my children, which would mean I'm the one responsible for them 95% of the time. They respect our decision, and they're quite happy with updates and photos of their grandkitties.

Who wouldn't be satisfied with pictures
of such adorable grandkitties?

DON'T YOU WANT A FAMILY?

I have one. I have a partner. I have a sibling. I have parents. I
have friends. I have pets. An absence of children is not an
absence of family.

YOU'RE BEING SELFISH.

So you think I'm selfish, but you want me to have kids? Make
it make sense.

DON'T YOU WANT TO GIVE YOUR PARTNER A CHILD?

If he wanted a child, I'd give him a divorce and let him find someone who also wanted a child.

It's not rocket science, y'all. I mean, do you really think childfree people are out here denying their partners children? And that their partners are just quietly suffering without kids because they're being cruelly deprived of them?

If someone wants a kid, it's their responsibility to find a partner who also wants one. If their partner doesn't want a kid, then they—being autonomous adults with brains and agency—need to decide what to do going forward. Do they stay and remain without children? Or do they leave and find someone who wants to be a parent?

It's not up to the childfree partner to give in and give their partner a child. It's up to the childless partner to grow up and make a decision for themselves. If they stay with a childfree partner, then *they are choosing to be childfree.*

r/RegretfulParents is *full* of stories from people who didn't want children, but their partners did, so they caved. It's especially common for women to give in to husbands who insist they'll share the work, but then it turns out Mom is doing 90% of the work anyway. So not only did she have a child she didn't want, but now she's saddled with most of the responsibility.

Don't pressure people to give their partner a child. If you're the partner who wants a child, take ownership and make a decision: stay and be childfree, or leave and have kids with someone else. Pressuring your partner into having a baby they don't want is never, ever okay, and I make no apologies for judging the hell out of you. Sorry not sorry.

And Lord, if you do persuade your partner to give you a child they don't want, you better step the hell up and be Parent of the Year *and* Partner of the Year.

Bottom line, you *cannot* compromise when it comes to having children. If you and your partner are mismatched in this department, then either someone is going to have to make a big sacrifice, or the relationship ends. If one of you wants children and the other doesn't, then love your partner enough to let them go so you can both find happiness elsewhere. I was prepared to do that when I told Eddie I didn't want kids. I hoped I didn't have to, and I'm grateful every day that I didn't, but if kids were a dealbreaker for him, then letting him go was the only solution that would've been kind to both of us. I would have sadly but willingly let him go if the happiness he deserved was with someone who also wanted kids.

It's really that simple. It's not easy, but it's simple.

Don't push someone who doesn't want kids into having them for someone else.

I know, I kind of went off on a tear on this one. Can you tell it drives me nuts?

BUT THE BIBLE SAID GO FORTH AND MULTIPLY.

You mean back when the earth's population was significantly lower than 8,000,000,000? When overpopulation, climate change, and all those fun things weren't issues? Yeah, I'm sure it did.

Meanwhile, here in 2024, the planet is not wanting for

human beings. Enough people have gone forth and multiplied that it's not going to hurt anyone if some of us decide not to.

And anyway, I couldn't begin to care less what the Bible says.

IF EVERYONE STOPS HAVING KIDS, HUMANS WILL GO EXTINCT!

Who said anything about "everyone"? Most people do have kids eventually. While more people than ever are childfree, there's hardly so many of us that diaper companies are going to go out of business.

Also, I think humans are far more likely to go extinct as a result of overpopulation than under, so...

THEN WHY DID YOU GET MARRIED?

Because I live in a society that incentivizes marriage with certain rights and privileges, including the right to make medical decisions for my spouse, the right to be at his bedside in the hospital, etc. Bonus: he was in the military, so being married meant we'd stay together when he was transferred.

Oh, and I also really love the guy, you know?

WHAT IF YOU MEET SOMEONE WHO WANTS KIDS?

I'm married to someone who doesn't want kids, so it's a moot point. Were I single, however, a person who wants kids wouldn't be the right person for me. It's really that simple.

YOU'LL CHANGE YOUR MIND.

Go back to page 1 and reread this whole book. Do it as many times as needed to understand why this is a stupid, rude, and presumptuous thing to say.

YOU'RE TOO YOUNG.

If I'm old enough to decide to have a baby, I'm old enough to decide not to. Period.

YOUR CHILD COULD CURE CANCER!

Well, so far, no one has cured cancer, and statistically, your kid is more likely to be a serial killer than win a Nobel Prize so... do you really want to risk it?

YOU SHOULD JUST HAVE ONE. IT'LL BE FINE.

This one. Ugh. This one. This attitude seriously cracks my gravy boat.

Kids are an enormous commitment. There's no refunds or take-backsies. What an absolutely appalling idea, that someone should just have a kid even when they've explicitly said they don't want one or they're not sure if they do. You can't just try it out, folks! Unless car dealerships have changed dramatically since I last bought a vehicle, you don't get to just test drive a new baby and then decide it's not for you.

I strongly believe parenthood is something people should

opt *into*, not out of. There's this pressure to just do it unless you can come up with an acceptable reason not to. I really, really believe it should be the other way around. Maybe we'd have fewer unhappy parents (and kids) if parents took the time to consciously decide *to* have children after considering why and why not.

YOU'LL REGRET IT.

I have never met a childfree by choice person who regrets it, but I've sure met some parents who do.

More importantly, I would much rather regret *not* having kids than regret having them. At least then I'm the only one who's affected by that regret.

CHAPTER 18

A FEW CLOSING WORDS

This isn't quite the last chapter. In the next, I have some advice for folks based on things I've seen, heard, and lived.

But this is where the memoir ends, so I wanted to include a few final thoughts. Mostly, I hope what readers take away is how important it is for us all to have open, honest dialogue about things. Our expectations in relationships. Our values and plans for the future. Our regrets and how we might have done things differently. As I've said throughout this book, one of the major influences that led me to become childfree was parents who were willing to be brutally honest about reality. They helped to paint a clearer picture of what parenthood entails, and that gave me the chance to rethink—from a place of being informed—if I really wanted that life.

It was also important for me to be brutally honest with myself. That isn't an easy process. None of us relish the idea of having difficult conversations with other people, but I would argue it's even harder to have those conversations with ourselves. It's daunting to put who we are under a microscope and really analyze what we do and do not want, what we are and are not wired for, and who we are and are not.

Sometimes this means a lot of quiet time thinking through everything. Sometimes it means challenging conversations with trusted friends, family, or even a therapist. Sometimes it's all of the above, followed by reality slapping you upside the head and refusing to let you continue to ignore the truth. Ask me how I know.

It's hard, but it's important.

Writing this book meant digging into some deep-seated trauma, and it stirred up a lot of emotions I haven't dealt with in a long time. It meant revisiting those old conversations with myself, and it also meant reliving experiences I would just as soon forget. I'm not going to tell you that was a fun process.

But you know what hit me harder than going through the infertility and pregnancy loss? What bothered me more than mentally reliving the losses?

Realizing how easily things could have played out differently.

I literally feel some low-grade panic every time I think about how I could have hesitated a *little* longer before trusting my feeling that I didn't want kids, gotten pregnant for real, and wound up a mother after all. It's like that feeling when you've nearly been in a car crash but managed to avoid getting hit—that jittery "oh, crap, things could have been so bad" feeling that sticks with you for a mile or two.

When I say I feel like I dodged a bullet by becoming childfree, I'm not being glib or snarky. I look at what parents deal with, what parenthood is like, and I genuinely believe from the bottom of my heart that I would have been a miserable parent. And I could have so, *so* easily become that miserable parent, but biology stepped in and bought me time. While I wouldn't wish infertility or pregnancy loss on anyone —while it was absolute hell to go through—the fact is that it's the reason I have the life I do now.

It's the reason I was able to become the person I am now. And just thinking about how quickly and easily my life could've been derailed by *staying on* the track I was on back then... legitimately makes my stomach somersault. When I read stories by parents who regret becoming parents, I feel it all the way to my core that I would've been writing those stories too.

We need, as a society, to talk about these things. With ourselves and with each other.

They say nothing can ever prepare you for the reality of becoming a parent, and yes, that's certainly true. There's only so much a person can glean from other people's experiences.

But that doesn't mean we shouldn't at least *try* to paint a realistic picture so people can make an informed decision and go into it with both eyes open. Talk about it. Talk about the good, the bad, and the ugly. If there's something you wish someone had told you before you had kids, don't keep it to yourself and let others find out the hard way. Talk about it.

Obviously, again, tact is important. Unsolicited advice is obnoxious regardless of intent. But if there are people in your life who are on the fence, or who are asking you what it's really like to have kids—people who want honest input before they make that commitment—*tell them.*

Throughout my journey, I heard a lot of parents say

things to the effect of, "I love my kids to hell and back, but I hate my life."

When they expanded on what it was they hated, it resonated with me. Lack of sleep. Lack of freedom. Lack of personal space. A type of love that felt a lot like anxiety.

At the end of the day, I didn't want to hate my life.

I made choices to live the life that sounded like one I wouldn't hate.

It isn't that parenthood is miserable and being childfree is amazing. It's that parenthood would be miserable *for me* and being childfree is amazing *for me*. For someone who knew she wanted to be a mother, my life would be awful. Likewise, as someone who knows I don't want to be a mother, that mother's life looks like the fifth circle of hell to me.

I think, as a culture, we need to start accepting that life is not one size fits all, and that includes the choice to procreate.

We accept that some people like a rural life while others prefer the suburbs or the city.

We accept that some people thrive in blue collar jobs while others are wired for white collar fields.

We accept that some people prefer dogs while others prefer cats.

But as a whole, society refuses to accept that parenthood is anything other than a universal biological imperative.

We refuse to accept that no one knows us better than we know ourselves.

Maya Angelou once said, "When someone shows you who they are, believe them the first time." This was, of course, in reference to people showing their true colors, but I think it's also applicable here. When someone *tells* you who they are, don't argue with them. Don't reject something they trusted you with. Don't undermine them and make them second guess their own decisions.

This applies—perhaps even more so—when that someone is you.

And when you hear a small voice inside yourself telling you who you are...

Stop and listen to it.

You just might learn something.

PART 5

OUTRO

Does this look like a kid who's worried about having a house full of cats? (pics by my parents)

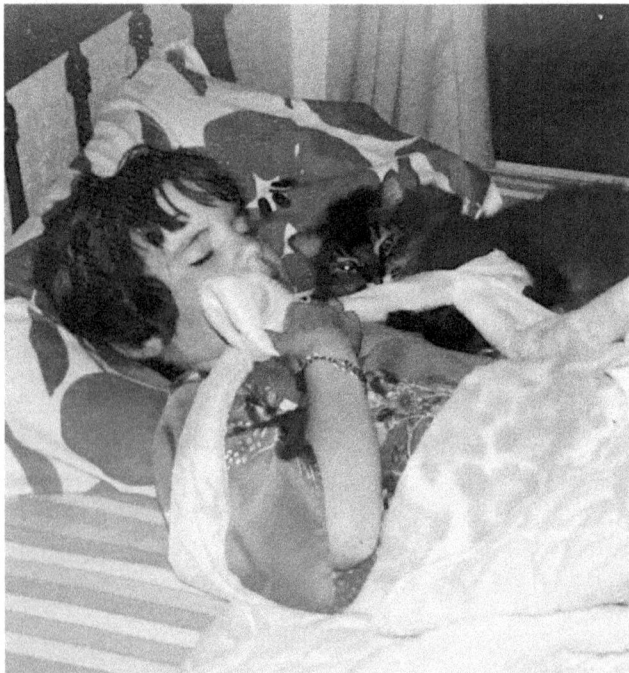

CHAPTER 19

MY ADVICE TO YOU

Having existed on both ends of the spectrum—from strug-gling with infertility all the way to *vehemently* childfree—I have insight into those experiences that are difficult to grasp if you haven't been there. People who've always been childfree aren't likely to fully understand the emotional gamut of someone going through infertility. Likewise, someone who has always wanted children might have difficulty getting their head around being adamantly against the idea of parenthood.

And then there are the people who are dead center—the fence sitters. Those who might or might not want kids. I've been there, too, so I'll offer up what I took away from that experience and what I've learned from being elsewhere on that spectrum.

I'm going to preface this by saying my experience is (obvi-ously) not universal. If something here doesn't resonate with you, that doesn't mean either of our experiences or insights are invalid. They're just different. I'm simply giving the advice and insights I can offer from my own experience at various places on the kids-or-no-kids spectrum. Take what works, and leave the rest.

With that out of the way, here we go!

TO THE CHILDFREE:

In all the years I've spent on childfree forums, there's one type of comment that pops up frequently and makes my teeth grind. I'll often see childfree people venting about how someone in their life is either complaining about infertility or grieving hard over a miscarriage, especially an early one.

I know for a lot of childfree folks, talking about trying for a baby is gross because someone is essentially announcing that they're having unprotected sex with their partner. I get it. But there is a cultural norm that people will discuss their plans for a family, if they're trying, etc., and that does extend to talking about fertility struggles. Sometimes it can be TMI. I totally understand that. And there isn't much I can say that will make it any less unsavory for childfree people to hear about or talk about, so I won't.

The advice I will offer is to extend a little bit of grace to people who are struggling with infertility or with pregnancy loss. I'm not asking you to let someone talk your ear off for hours on end about something you find uncomfortable. Boundaries are important. All I'm asking is for folks to understand that the grief and all the other emotions that accompany infertility and loss are real and difficult. Sometimes people in your circles will seek support, and even if babies and pregnancy are miles out of your wheelhouse... at least be kind.

For people who have never wanted children—especially those who are repulsed by the idea—it is understandably difficult to imagine the emotions involved with infertility and pregnancy loss. I promise you, though, that it is incredibly hard and very taxing for them. No one experiences life the same way, and both sides of this coin—feeling those emotions relating to infertility or miscarriages and not understanding those emotions—are valid.

Protracted struggles with infertility are *miserable*. Imagine working toward something that's deeply important to you, especially something that seems to come relatively easily to people around you. Now imagine that something being kept out of your reach. There's no real definitive reason, and every solution is physically painful, emotionally draining, and prohibitively expensive. People in your circles inexplicably obtain it with ease, but for you, there are barriers in place that you might not even be able to define, never mind overcome. Imagine feeling like an enormous part of your life is on hold until you can finally overcome those barriers.

That's what it feels like, and to be blunt, it sucks. Even now, when the idea of getting pregnant and having a baby prompts a full-throated *"HELL NO"* from me, I vividly remember how miserable infertility was.

And pregnancy losses—those are awful. While it's easy for some to dismiss as losing a clump of cells rather than a fully-formed baby, especially in the early weeks, it's really not that simple. The grief is very, very real. On top of that, the physical process can be incredibly painful, and the hormone crash is hell. As I mentioned in a previous chapter, I learned the hard way that postpartum depression can happen even after an early miscarriage, and it's completely separate from grief and other emotions. It's a *beast*.

You don't have to empathize with why any of these struggles are hard or why the person feels the way they do. You don't have to have firsthand knowledge of what it feels like. You don't even have to understand on a rational level how they feel or why.

Just be kind. That's all.

What you do or say depends entirely on the kind of relationship you have with the person and with your comfort zone. Maybe you're close enough to offer a shoulder and listen. Maybe just saying, "I'm sorry you're going through that" is enough. Even just quietly giving them time and grace, understanding that they might be out of sorts for a period of time or they might be physically recovering. No one's expecting grand gestures or for the childfree to swoop in and heroically help people through.

Literally just be kind, even if you don't understand or can't relate to what they're going through.

TO THE FENCE SITTERS:

This is not an easy position to be in, and I don't envy you. I'm not going to offer any advice to nudge you in either direction because that isn't my place. Some of what I talk about here will skew childfree because that's the way I ultimately went; I'm not unbiased and I don't pretend to be. What I will do is be as balanced as I can and offer up some of the thought processes I went through while I was sitting on the fence.

One thing I learned in observing other parents is that you won't change as much as you think after having a baby. Your priorities will shift, of course, and your life will change dramatically.

But wherever you go, there you are, and even with a baby in your arms, you're still the person you were before.

What I mean by this is quite simply that a baby does change what's expected and required of you, but it doesn't magically change *you*.

There's a meme floating around that says something to the effect of, "All my New Year's resolutions hinge upon me suddenly becoming a very different person tomorrow." In other words, people will resolve to clean their house better, get up earlier, go to the gym, stick to a schedule, grocery shop wisely, and cook from scratch... despite knowing full well they're a person who struggles to do even one of those things.

Can it be done? Sure! But it's a lot harder for someone who isn't already the early riser who cooks from scratch and goes to the gym.

If you have problems with executive dysfunction now, that isn't going to go away now that you have a baby who needs to be bathed, fed, changed, burped, put down for naps, etc., over and over and over again. Especially on top of all the other tasks you already struggle with and while you're sleep-deprived.

Again, can it be done? Absolutely. But be honest with yourself about who you are, who you need to be with a baby, and whether you'll be comfortable in the shoes you'll need to wear. The answer may be yes. It may be no.

My advice is simply to take a good, hard look at yourself, and if you *do* decide to have a baby, go into it with open eyes and realistic expectations of yourself. If you have a baby and don't suddenly turn into the flawless 1950s sitcom parent, give yourself grace. If your house was kind of cluttered before the baby, and it's still cluttered after the baby, you're not a failure. If your laundry piled up until you ran out of underwear before, and now you have a precarious mountain of clothes needing to be washed, it's okay. Cut yourself some slack.

The "you're not going to change as much as you think" applies in a lot of other ways, too. Things you don't like now, you're not going to magically like as a parent. If you're not someone who likes to be touched a lot, you're probably going to be touched out. If you're noise reactive and can't deal with crying or screaming, that's not going to change when the crying and screaming is *your* responsibility and there's *no* escape.

Do those things mean you shouldn't be a parent? Only you can decide that. Only you can decide if the payoff—the pros of having children—are worthwhile.

For me, they're not. I think I could've been a good parent, but I couldn't honestly convince myself I'd be a *happy* parent or a *fulfilled* parent. I don't think there's anything wrong with realizing and acknowledging that. I think it's perfectly acceptable to say, "The person I am wouldn't be happy as a parent, and the kids I'd have wouldn't be happy with me as a parent." It's also okay to say, "I acknowledge that I'll struggle with these things, but I believe they'll be worthwhile, so I'm going to have kids."

I think the most important thing is simply to be honest with yourself about who you are and what you want. If that flowchart leads you to having children, then I wish you the best of luck. If it leads you to the childfree life, then I also wish you the best of luck.

The other piece of advice I would offer is, when people pressure you one way or the other, to take a step back and scrutinize *why* they're giving you that advice. Is it coming from a genuine desire to see you happy and fulfilled? Or is there an ulterior motive? Are they speaking from a spiritual or religious path that you don't share, pressuring you to fall into step with something you might not believe in? (Yep, that one happens—I've had people who know full well I'm an atheist unironically push me toward motherhood because "It's what God intends")

Don't let yourself be swayed by people who have their own agenda or are projecting their own regrets, desires, and values on you. Don't let someone use a subjective opinion as an objective truth and scare you into something you don't want.

For example, when people declare to you that if you don't have children, you'll be alone and miserable in your twilight years before you finally die, at which point your cats will eat you. Kids aren't the only company or support networks people have, and they're not guaranteed anyway.

For whatever reason, the latest scare tactic is that you'll turn 40, realize you're alone except for your cats, and have nothing but regrets. Y'all, I'm 43. Yes, I do have cats, but I'm also happily married, and I have a broad support network of friends and family. I'm not lonely and I don't regret the choice I made a decade and a half ago, not even with peri-menopause kicking in and letting me know that time is very quickly running out (though not quickly enough—hurry *up*, Mother Nature).

Whatever choice you ultimately make, I urge you to make it based on your values, your personality, your wants, and your needs, not those projected on you by other people.

TO THE INFERTILE:

I'm not going to tell you that you should or shouldn't continue trying to get pregnant, or that you should become childfree, or that you should adopt. It isn't my place to tell you any of those things, and I truly do wish you the best in whichever path you choose. Infertility is hard—I genuinely hope it resolves in a way that brings you peace, and that you can be happy and content going forward.

What I *will* suggest is, during your infertility journey, to make sure you don't lose yourself.

A lot of mothers express frustration that as soon as they become moms, that's all they become. They struggle to be anything but Mom. I would argue that that can begin well before there's a baby or even a positive pregnancy test. Infertility can become all-consuming, and it is startling how quickly and completely it can take over a person's identity.

It's okay to still find joy in life while you're struggling with infertility. It's okay to still be happy. It's okay to have hobbies and interests, and to put time and energy into those interests. I know that sounds like common sense—like seriously, who's stopping you?—but I remember from my own experience and from observing others that it's surprisingly easy to get swallowed up by it. To deny yourself any joy or fulfilment that isn't directly tied to becoming a parent. Like even if you're doing the things you want to, you refuse to *allow* them to fulfill you because you don't feel like anything *will* or *should* other than defeating infertility.

Don't do that to yourself. Let yourself breathe even when it feels like you're only allowed to suffocate. Let yourself be happy even while you're going through something miserable. Let yourself be *you*.

Your mental health is going to take a hit from infertility. That seems to be an almost universal experience. It's frustrating to watch everyone around you having kids while you're failing Applied Biology 101 (as I used to describe it for myself because I cope by making fun of everything). It's hard not to feel like a failure (spoiler: you're not a failure). It's hard not to think time is running out (it's really not—your eggs don't dry up the day you turn 35). It's aggravating and hurtful to get interrogated by well-meaning (and not) people who have invested themselves in your reproductive abilities.

All around, it sucks. 0/10, do not recommend.

And maneuvering through all of that is *going* to take its toll on your mental health.

Remember to take care of *you*. Talk to a therapist if you need to. Find friends or relatives who respect your boundaries, whether that means letting you vent sometimes or not bringing up the infertility issues unless you do. Make sure you have friends who exist *outside* of infertility.

One of my friends was struggling with secondary infertility, and we spent a lot of time together largely because I wouldn't ask about it. That wasn't to say she couldn't talk about it with me—I was certainly happy to be there for her!—but our friendship existed outside of that. She gravitated toward me because we didn't talk about toddlers or potty training or infertility. We talked about our careers, the places we liked traveling to, and our hobbies. We talked about *life*.

When I was going through infertility myself, I had a number of people I could talk to about other things. For example, my coworker Naomi. While we could talk about kids and such, we usually didn't. We talked about workouts and weight training. We vented about work and random things we heard on the radio during our commutes. At the same time, the option was there to talk about the things that were frustrating me, just as we could talk about the things going on in her world, but we could also just be *friends*.

Make sure you hold on to that—to friendships and relationships where your life and theirs continue and thrive even while you're trying to have a baby.

Also, speaking of relationships, most people struggling with infertility aren't doing it alone. Don't forget your partner. They should be your support, and you should also be supporting them. Check in with each other. If it's taking a toll on your relationship, it's okay to put a pin in the infertility struggle and just be a couple for a while.

And when I say "put a pin in the fertility struggle and just be a couple for a while," I don't mean "let's stop trying, wink, wink, because that's when it'll probably happen." People will absolutely give you that advice, and you can gaslight yourself into thinking you're taking a break when you're really just pretending you're not trying. You'll still be stressed out.

I mean... *stop* trying for a little while. Even if it's just a month, or a weekend getaway. Use protection and actively *don't* try. Give yourself and your partner space to just be together and be a couple instead of everything circling back to the elephant in the nursery. Taking a short breather isn't going to send you back to square one.

Hold on to your identity as an individual, make sure your partner is doing the same, and hold on to your identity as a couple. You don't want to get to the end of things, have a baby, and then realize you and your partner don't know each other or yourselves anymore. When you finally have that baby, you'll be at the end of the line with your fertility specialists. Don't be at the end of the line with your partner, too. Have a relationship that exists—wholly and happily —*outside* of your infertility.

Notice the constant drumbeat here is to exist *outside* of your infertility. It's hard to put out of your mind sometimes— believe me, I know—but I highly recommend keeping your-self anchored in a world that isn't defined by ovulation, hormones, and longing for a positive test. Have things to look forward to and be excited about, and don't feel guilty for enjoying your life even while you're dealing with infertility.

TO THE MILITARY SPOUSES...

It's become a stereotype that we marry young and immedi-ately start having babies. There's even a running joke on some of the bases that there's something in the water (I stuck to Dr Pepper on Okinawa, just to be safe).

In all seriousness, though, it really is common for young military couples to become young military parents. People get caught up in being newlyweds.

They also get excited about all the military benefits, and I'm dead serious about that part. Now that you're married to the military, you've got free healthcare and access to military medical facilities. When you hear about civilian couples being slapped with five-figure bills after uncomplicated deliveries, there is a sense of urgency to have all your babies while you're still covered by TriCare. Especially with couples where the service member isn't planning to stay in for more than a few years, the clock is ticking!

And quite bluntly, sometimes it seems like there isn't much else to do but have babies. The military spouse community is mostly moms, and it's hard to find a place in that community if you don't have kids. I've had more than a few milspouses look askance at me when I said I didn't want kids. My husband was on active duty for the first nineteen years of our marriage, and I can count on one hand the number of milspouses with whom I made any lasting connection. I just never found a place within that community. Some of that was because I was focused on my career and admittedly could be a bit reclusive, but also because I simply never felt like part of the group. When I attended military functions, I sometimes ended up sitting with some of the wives, and the conversation would be solely about babies and kids. That got increasingly isolating over time; eventually, I gave up and tried to hang out with my husband and the guys just because I didn't want to hear another story involving ultrasounds, episiotomies, or tantrums.

The milspouse life is not easy. There are some great perks and benefits, but the tradeoff is a lot of uncertainty and upheaval. Isolation and loneliness are very common.

With all of that being said, my advice to you is not to let your experience as a milspouse determine if or when you have children.

TO PEOPLE WHO HAVE LOVED ONES STRUGGLING WITH INFERTILITY...

I know most of y'all mean well, and I'm not pretending that you're being malicious.

That being said, let me set the record straight:

A lot of your advice and encouragement is far less welcome than you think.

Some of the most well-intended comments I received during that period of my life were also some of the most hurtful and intrusive. It didn't matter if they weren't intended to be that way—that was how they hit. And they really, really did hurt. Especially because most people didn't seem to realize they weren't the *only* ones issuing that advice or those comments.

To be clear, I'm not talking about when your loved one is asking for advice. I'm specifically talking about the people who insinuate themselves into someone's infertility struggle with unsolicited advice.

- **"Have you tried... (chiropractic,**

meditation, IVF, this MLM's overpriced supplement, suppositories created from crystallized pine needles from the eastern slope of this one specific mountain in Mongolia, etc.)?" If we don't know each other well enough for me to have already told you what I've tried, then you are probably overstepping by asking.

- **"You and your husband should try—"** Nope. Stop. *Cease.* If it wouldn't be appropriate for you to comment on this person's sex life under normal circumstances, it's not appropriate to discuss it in terms of infertility.

- **"You're just overthinking it and stressing yourself out."** The only way for a person to really defend themselves here—which they shouldn't have to do—is to disclose private medical information. Don't put people in a position where they feel they have to prove they have something legitimately wrong. Also, there is already a ton of guilt associated with infertility, especially if there have been losses along the way; insinuating that it's their fault is beyond rude—it's cruel.

Every well-meaning comment has the potential to be a serious emotional minefield. It's a stressful thing to go through, and there are a lot of emotions involved (guilt, shame, anger, grief, frustration). But it's also not socially acceptable for people to be rude to those offering unsolicited advice and platitudes, so the fact that someone just smiles and thanks you instead of enforcing a boundary doesn't mean your comments are welcome. Oftentimes it's a way of avoiding confrontation and moving on from the subject because they're uncomfortable.

Personally, I *despise* unsolicited advice as a general rule, but I get a lot of it. It got to the point I started ending social media posts with *"No advice, please,"* and even that earned me lectures and backlash. People still respond with "This isn't advice, but...(advice)." When I push back, they get offended and tell me I'm being rude and that they're just trying to be helpful. It's *extraordinarily* difficult to set that boundary and enforce it because it isn't socially acceptable.

As a result, when you offer unsolicited or intrusive advice, you're putting the other person into a very uncomfortable position of not being able to tell you if they're uncomfortable for fear of being the bad guy for making *you* uncomfortable.

This applies to everything, not just infertility; it just happens to be a really difficult and uncomfortable thing when someone is infertile. They're already going through something awful, plus it's a very intimate topic, and society discourages them from setting and enforcing boundaries, so they have to either pretend it doesn't bother them or risk causing a scene.

How can you tell if that's what they're doing? How can you tell if someone is truly thankful for your advice versus smiling and nodding in hopes that you'll let the subject drop? Well, that's a tough one.

My advice (I know, irony) is to *ask*.

- "I'd love to be able to help, but is this something you want to talk about?"
- "I know some people who've been through this; would you be interested in hearing about their experiences?"
- "I know this can be a very uncomfortable topic; I have some thoughts you might find helpful, but I'll understand if it isn't something you want to discuss. Would you like to hear them?"

Ask these questions *genuinely*, too, and read the room. Are they saying "yes" to be polite? Or do they really want to talk about it?

If you're not sure, or if you don't know the person well enough to gauge if they're interested versus being polite... then it's worth considering that you don't know them well enough to proceed with this conversation.

I know this sounds harsh and even abrasive, and again, I know most people are well-intentioned. But it's important to keep boundaries and comfort in mind. It's very easy for someone who's pregnant or trying to conceive to suddenly feel like their life and bodily autonomy are public property; when others start verbally probing into incredibly intimate and painful territory—it sucks!

I'm not out to make people feel attacked or like they can't speak, but I hope it'll cause some folks to rethink how they approach people experiencing infertility. Because whatever discomfort you're getting from reading this, I assure you, it's a lot less than the discomfort experienced by the infertile person grinning and bearing it through yet another well-meaning person discussing their sex life, their body, their diet, and their medical history.

Finally, one thing that came up on infertility boards and in conversations with infertile people is the almost universal hatred of, *"Stop trying, and then it'll happen!"*

It really doesn't matter what your intent is when you say that. It doesn't matter that you know someone who gave up and instantly got pregnant. None of that matters because it's not about you. It's about a cheerfully dismissive remark directed at someone who is going through hell.

Please, please, don't say those words to someone experiencing infertility.

TO ANYONE WHO QUESTIONS SOMEONE ELSE'S FAMILY PLANS...

While we're on the subject of well-meaning but intrusive folks, it is incredibly common for people to grill others about their family plans.

- "What do you mean, you don't want kids?"
- "Instead of going through those treatments, why not adopt?"
- "Instead of adopting, why not try getting treated? Medical technology has come a long way!"
- "You're stopping at one? Don't you want to give him a sibling?"
- "You're stopping at two boys? Don't you want to

try for a girl?"
- "Don't you think four is enough?"
- "Six kids, huh? You know what causes that, right?"

You get the idea. No matter what choices people make regarding their family size, there will always be people who question them.

If you're one of those people who asks or has asked those questions... please. Stop. Even if you mean well, it's really none of your business, and you're probably not the only person who has asked or will ask those questions.

I've been both the infertile person and the childfree person getting intrusive questions, and it sucks. Please, regardless of your intent... stop.

And if you're shaking your head and dismissing this advice because the person in question is your adult child or child-in-law... it does apply to you. It applies to you a lot. You should be a safe, trusted part of your child or their spouse's journey, not a source of stress or frustration. You made your own reproductive decisions. Now it's their turn. Butt out, be respectful, mind their boundaries, or make peace with a future involving the words "no contact."

TO ANYONE WHO'S TIRED OF BEING POLITE TO PEOPLE WHO GIVE UNSOLICITED ADVICE OR QUESTION YOUR FAMILY PLANS...

Set boundaries and enforce them. If necessary, be rude and don't apologize for it.

If someone says you're making them uncomfortable—no, you are *responding* to being *made* uncomfortable. It's not a childish *"You started it!"*, either; it's the consequences of *their* words and actions. Fuck around and find out, as they say.

If you've ever been to the subreddit Am I The Asshole?, you've probably seen that a good 80% of the posts boil down to, *"Someone did something toxic/abusive/cruel/rude, and I stood my ground. Now everyone's mad at me. Am I the asshole?"*

I'm out of patience with that. I also know it's hard to stand up to people sometimes, especially when they're your boss, an older relative, or what have you. But I think more of us should start matching energy. We shouldn't have to be polite to those who hurt us. We shouldn't have to smile through it just because they have good intentions.

Whether you're childfree, infertile, or anyone in between, you don't owe anyone politeness when they question you about things that are none of their business. You don't owe anyone answers, and you absolutely don't owe anyone explanations for those answers.

There is absolutely nothing wrong with a firm, "My decision is made and I'm not going to discuss it any further." If someone pushes—and I don't care who that someone is—then you are well within your rights to walk away, tell them off, ignore them, block them, etc.

If anyone says you're rude for doing that, tell them you have my permission. If they ask what involvement I have in the situation, tell them, "As much involvement as you have in my family planning."

AND FINALLY, TO THE ASPIRING WRITERS...

You can do it. I believe in you.

If people try to discourage you and you're struggling to keep going, push through anyway—succeed for yourself, but also for the sweet, sweet satisfaction of proving your naysayers wrong.

When all else fails, spite is a hell of a drug.

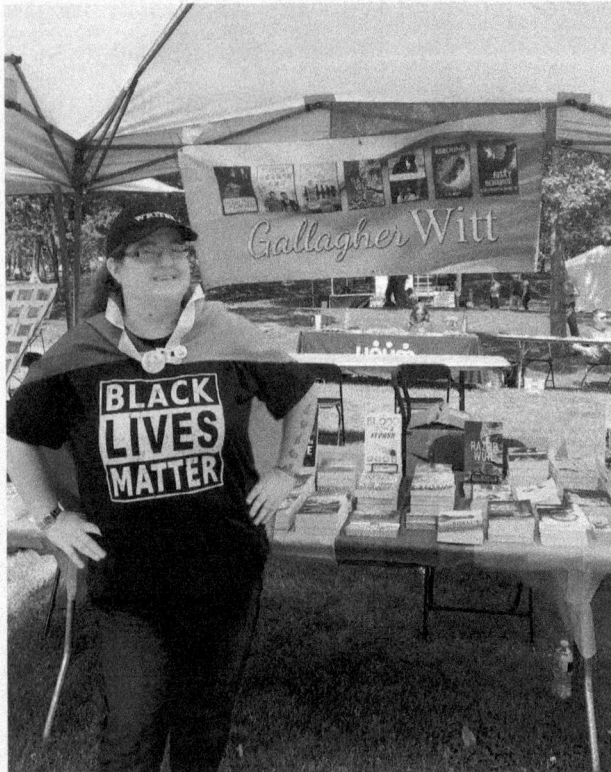

Me, selling books at Bangor Pride, Bangor, Maine, 2019.

NOTES

8. ANCHORS AWEIGH

1. PCS stands for Permanent Change of Station. Essentially, being transferred from one duty station to the next. Service members and families use the acronym as a verb. "We're about to PCS." "We PCSed here from San Diego." "When are you PCSing?" etc.

11. AUTHOR AT LAST

1. The Big Five publishers are the major New York publishing houses: Penguin/Random House, Simon and Schuster, Hachette, MacMillan, and HarperCollins.

13. OLD ENOUGH TO GET PREGNANT

1. Vasectomies are reasonably reversible, but the doctor's point was that a person shouldn't get one with the assumption that they'd just have it reversed later. It should be approached as a permanent procedure, not something that could be easily undone down the line.

For more books by L.A. Witt, or to subscribe to my newsletter, please visit

http://www.gallagherwitt.com

Newsletter perks:

- Exclusive discounts & giveaways
- Access to ARCs
- All the latest news about pre-orders, collaborations, and more!

Romance * Suspense

Contemporary * Historical * Sports * Military

Titles Include

Rookie Mistake (written with Anna Zabo)

Scoreless Game (written with Anna Zabo)

The Hitman vs. Hitman Series (written with Cari Z)

The Bad Behavior Series (written with Cari Z)

The Gentlemen of the Emerald City Series

The Anchor Point Series

The Husband Gambit

Name From a Hat Trick

After December

Brick Walls

The Venetian and the Rum Runner

If The Seas Catch Fire

...and many, many more!

ABOUT THE AUTHOR

L.A. Witt is a romance and suspense author who has at last given up the exciting nomadic lifestyle of the military spouse (read: her husband finally retired). She now resides in Pittsburgh, where the potholes are determined to eat her car and her cats are endlessly taunted by a disrespectful squirrel named Moose. In her spare time, she can be found painting in her art room or destroying her voice at a Pittsburgh Penguins game.

Website: www.gallagherwitt.com
    Email: gallagherwitt@gmail.com
    Twitter: @GallagherWitt

www.ingramcontent.com/pod-product-compliance
Lightning Source LLC
Chambersburg PA
CBHW051823040426
42447CB00006B/345